You ARE What You THINK

Basic Issues in Pastoral Counseling

You ARE What You THINK

Basic Issues in Pastoral Counseling

Robert C. Brien

Regular Baptist Press
Post Office Box 95500
1300 North Meacham Road
Schaumburg, Illinois 60195

Library of Congress Cataloging-in-Publication Data

Brien, Robert C., 1926-
    You are what you think.

    Bibliography: p.
    Includes index.
    1. Pastoral counseling. I. Title.
BV4012.2.B736   1986   253.5   86-460
ISBN 0-87227-102-1

YOU ARE WHAT YOU THINK:
BASIC ISSUES IN PASTORAL COUNSELING
© 1986
Regular Baptist Press
Schaumburg, Illinois
Printed in U.S.A.

Contents

Foreword

The need for pastoral counseling in the church appears to be growing exponentially. Yet few pastors have received adequate training in the field and, indeed, few seminaries provide such training. In addition, there is a dearth of reliable, Scripturally based and yet professionally competent books from which a pastor may learn the basic tools of counseling. Most books on counseling published within recent years have been of little practical value to the pastor. Indeed, some of them have proposed methods and techniques that not only are inadequate but sometimes dangerous for the counselee.

It is a fact of life today that Christians may be affected with all the maladies to which human flesh is heir and that we will retain this potential until the day we are received into Glory. To deny such a reality may in itself be a manifestation of emotional disorder. To claim that there is no need for vitamins because we have Jesus is to say that we never need deodorants because He is the Rose of Sharon. Such thinking speaks for itself.

Dr. Brien has done an inestimable service to the Bible-believing church and to pastors who are seeking to understand the distresses of parishioners and to provide rationally based, Scripturally consistent and effective help. Everything he says is based squarely on the Scriptures as the divinely inspired and inerrant Word of God, which forever remains the ultimate authority in all we seek and do. With Scripture as the base, Dr. Brien provides us with an excellent review of the basic questions that confront the pastor-counselor in both theory and practice.

He outlines the value, strategies and techniques of the rational-cognitive approach in which he himself was tutored by Dr.

Maxie Maultsby of the Rational Behavior Therapy Institute of the University of Kentucky at Louisville. The great advantage of the Rational Behavior Therapy approach is that it is learned relatively easily, and experience has proven it to be a very successful approach to helping people with a variety of emotional difficulties help themselves. In my opinion, Rational Behavior Therapy, when based on a Scriptural foundation, is one of the most useful and reliable tools available to the pastor-counselor. It enables a rapid diagnosis to be made of the basic problems and then clearly points in the direction in which therapy should proceed.

Every pastor who seeks to help hurting people will find much that is both useful and practical in this approach from a professional point of view. At the same time, he can rest assured that the approach is thoroughly consistent with the Word of God. We are in Dr. Brien's debt.

Basil Jackson, M.D., Ph.D., Th.D.

Introduction

This book was written because of the interest I have had in pastoral counseling since seminary days when I wrote a research paper entitled "Cause and Cure of Mental Illness." As a young minister in Pontiac, Michigan, I found myself involved one afternoon a week visiting various patients in the Michigan State Mental Hospital. Without technical training in the field of counseling but with a confidence in the love, power and Word of God, I saw some dramatic successes with some very distressed patients.

Through more than twenty-eight years of doing "ordinary" pastoral counseling (similar to Jay Adams's Nouthetic Counseling), some glaring failures showed me the need to better understand the way the human mind functions. I might then better apply the resources of God in meeting desperate emotional needs. Discussions with my son, David, who has a degree in psychology from the University of Wisconsin, have also encouraged my interest in this field.

However, perhaps the strongest influence in my life concerning pastoral counseling was my training in Rational Behavior Therapy (RBT) at Milwaukee Lutheran Hospital under Dr. Maultsby in the fall of 1976. During that training, my "practice patient" (a man who I later discovered had a Ph.D. in psychology) told me that he had learned more about himself in a one-and-a-half hour session of RBT than in all his years of training and practice.

Dr. Basil Jackson of the Jackson Psychiatric Clinic, a born-again Christian and professor at the Medical College of Wisconsin, encouraged me to take the RBT training. Later, Dr. Jackson was my instructor for several courses in graduate school and also my advisor for my doctoral dissertation upon which this book is largely based. His wide training in both psychology and theology has been of inestimable value to me.

Though many books and articles have been written about pastoral counseling, none seem to deal with the basic issues and presuppositions of pastoral counseling in a systematic, concise and Scriptural manner. Most of these books deal primarily with types of cases or types and techniques of counseling. It is my purpose to provide prospective pastor-counselors with a concise overview of the basic issues of counseling and to recommend one particular method of counseling, a modified form of RBT. This method is fairly easily learned and makes both theological and psychological sense to me. However, I do recognize that all techniques for uncovering the unconscious and therapeutic approaches that do not contradict the Scriptures should be understood and employed at the pastor's discretion. The RBT framework lends itself easily to the use of these many other insights. It also allows room for the application of every Scriptural doctrine or principle of which I am aware.

For many years we have been made increasingly aware that what we eat vitally affects our physical well-being. Recently it has been discovered that various food substances even influence brain functions. Foods can affect our moods, alertness, memory and even our perception of pain. Those researchers who contend that we are what we eat certainly have much evidence to substantiate their view. But it is my conviction that **what we are is determined even more by our thinking than by our eating.** What we are has more to do with the condition of our minds than with the condition of our bodies.

The view that we are what we think is not new; it goes back at least as far as Solomon who said, "As [a man] thinketh in his heart, so is he" (Prov. 23:7). Ancient thinkers such as Epictetus, Titus and Marcus Aurelius were proponents of the same idea.

In recent years secular psychiatrists and psychologists such as Albert Ellis, Maxie Maultsby, A. T. Beck and David Burns (whose book *Feeling Good* I highly recommend) have been advocating the cognitive (or thinking) approach to mental distress. More and more the cognitive approach is showing through in the writings of several Christian psychologists. William Backus's book *Telling Yourself the Truth* is an excellent application from the Christian perspective of the cognitive approach to several types of mental illness.

Some believe that our thoughts can be our best friends and our worst enemies. One's thoughts embrace every area of one's being: physical health (thinking can result in headaches, backaches, tiredness, ulcers, colitis, high blood pressure, allergies, stroke, heart disease and even some forms of cancer); interpersonal relationships—especially his relationship with God; happiness (which depends upon how much or little he demands or expects of himself and others); ability to effectively communicate (what he is thinking influences the way he says things and how he hears them); economic well-being (some perceive themselves to be losers and therefore become losers); status as a law-abiding citizen or as a criminal; freedom from or addiction to the clock (how a person thinks about time can kill him); and ability to break free or remain free from the bondage of alcohol, tobacco or overeating.

I trust that this book will clarify the basic issues of pastoral counseling. Perhaps then many pastors who have been reluctant to train in this field will learn to use Scriptural and psychological principles in a way that is honoring to the Lord and that will bring relief to burdened hearts.

Robert C. Brien

1 The Confusion Concerning Pastoral Counseling

Perplexing questions

The following perplexing questions have frightened many a pastor away from a ministry of counseling. By facing these questions squarely, it is hoped that many more pastors will prepare themselves for this ministry, the need of which is likely to increase in the future. Some of these questions will be answered briefly here; others will be dealt with in later chapters.

Are Christian theology and psychology compatible? A major question is, How do psychological discoveries agree with Biblical teaching?

The seeming antagonism between theology and psychology is not based on the psychological discoveries themselves. It is based on the *interpretations* of these discoveries which are influenced by psychologists' educational and religious backgrounds and personal values.

Some secular psychologists have blamed the Christian religion for bringing about emotional disturbances. Others claim that they have succeeded in explaining away religious experience. Still others admit that they can neither fully explain religious experience nor tell us whether or not it is of God. And certainly the counsel of some in the area of morals has been in conflict with the teachings of Jesus Christ.

A few decades ago some secular psychologists began to see the value of having ministers on their healing teams. However, the ministers' contribution was not recognized as being primary. Today more and more psychologists are concluding that Christian principles are of primary importance in relieving burdened souls.

All truth is God's truth, and His truth in psychology will certainly agree with His truth in the Scriptures. Collins states that discipleship counseling "assumes that the God who speaks through the Bible has also revealed truth about His universe through science, including psychology."[1]

After several years of tension, there is now a much greater and refreshing openness and sharing between Biblical theology and psychology. In fact there have been several attempts to integrate them. An increasing number of people trained in psychology and psychiatry unashamedly embrace Biblical Christianity and their methods are compatible with their faith. Such an increase certainly has done much to remove the hostility between psychology and theology. And there is also a growing awareness among those trained in theology that religious experience must be mediated by psychological processes.

When these disciplines appear to be in conflict, it is either because our knowledge of psychology is partial or faulty or because we have not rightly interpreted the Scripture. Psychology and theology, when properly understood, are being seen more and more as allies rather than enemies. I believe that not one principle of Christianity has to be sacrificed in order for it to be compatible with the facts of psychology. There are, then, no necessary tensions between Christian theology and psychology.

Will an emphasis on a healthy state of mind produce self-centeredness and a focus on earthly happiness? Recent thinking in the fields of philosophy, psychology and religion seems to point to a new and greater emphasis upon one's earthly life and happiness. This emphasis has focused attention upon man's emotional life and upon the psychological principles that man thinks will help him achieve earthly happiness. Our age seems to be caught up in what Freud called "primary narcissism."

Theodore Roszak, an observer of America's counterculture,

believes that America is launched on "the biggest introspective binge any society in history has undergone."[2]

In his book *The Universe Next Door: A Basic World View Catalog* James Sire describes Carlos Castanedas's new consciousness philosophy as a conception that places the human self at the center of all reality.[3]

Marvin Stone, the editor of *U.S. News & World Report,* decries our "sad solipsist" society in a September 5, 1978 editorial. He explains:

> It goes also by less-technical names, among them "self-fulfillment," "the 'me' culture," "the new narcissism," hedonism and plain selfishness. It has been attributed to "the 'me' generation," but that is not entirely accurate since the fever attacks persons of all ages.[4]

He goes on to say, "Self-fulfillment, to the exclusion of all else, is self-delusion."[5]

Martin Gross says:

> We live in a civilization in which as never before, man is preoccupied with "self." We have become fascinated with our madness, motivations and our endless, sometimes wearying search for normality. Modern psychology and psychiatry seek to satisfy that fascination by offering us a full range of systems, from the serious to the whimsical, with which we can understand our confused psyche, then seek to heal it.[6]

The new psychologies that put the main emphasis upon feeling, peak experiences or self-actualizations are other examples of self-centeredness. These are the psychotherapies that stress doing your own thing and letting it all hang out.

The growing emphasis upon the healthy state of the mind is generally an indication of self-centeredness and of an overemphasis upon happiness in this life, but not always. And even if it is, it provides an opportunity for the pastor-counselor to deal faithfully but tactfully with this self-centeredness. Since a pastor's time is limited, he needs the discernment of the Lord to determine when a counselee is making excessive demands upon his time.

It must be admitted that some seek pastoral counseling for

selfish reasons. But people also go to dentists, physicians and even church for selfish reasons. Many troubled believers are not only concerned about themselves but are also concerned about the testimony of their lives. They want to enjoy the abundant life Jesus promised, and they want their lives to be attractive to the unconverted to influence them for Christ.

Are the Word of God and the Spirit of God sufficient resources for meeting psychological needs? It is clearly evident that mental problems that originate in brain damage or defect or in body chemistry will not be helped any more by the Word of God than would a case of gallstones. The Word of God and the Spirit of God can, of course, enable such a person to better live with his condition.

When one accepts that all psychopathology is related to wrong thinking, especially to self-deceit, then one can see how the resources of God can help solve such problems. The Bible does teach that divine resources can literally transform a man's thinking, feelings and actions:

> And be not conformed to this world: but be ye transformed by the renewing of your mind, that ye may prove what is that good, and acceptable, and perfect, will of God (Rom. 12:2).

> Therefore if any man be in Christ, he is a new creature: old things are passed away; behold, all things are become new (2 Cor. 5:17).

> This I say then, Walk in the Spirit, and ye shall not fulfill the lust of the flesh. . . . But the fruit of the Spirit is love, joy, peace, longsuffering, gentleness, goodness, faith. Meekness, temperance: against such there is no law (Gal. 5:16, 22, 23).

> For it is God which worketh in you both to will and to do of his good pleasure (Phil. 2:13).

> All scripture is given by inspiration of God, and is profitable for doctrine, for reproof, for correction, for instruction in righteousness (2 Tim. 3:16).

> According as his divine power hath given unto us all things that pertain unto life and godliness, through the knowledge of him that hath called us to glory and virtue: Whereby are given unto us exceeding great and precious promises: that by these ye might

be partakers of the divine nature, having escaped the corruption that is in the world through lust (2 Pet. 1:3, 4).

For as he thinketh in his heart, so is he. . . . (Prov. 23:7a).

It is also true that the counsel of ungodly men can transform man's thinking, feelings and actions. Here the Christian's presuppositions based upon the Word of God become the criteria of what is real and therefore reasonable. We need to heed the warning of O. H. Mowrer who asked, "Has evangelical Christianity [in failing to use the Bible] sold its birthright for a mess of pottage?"[7]

What, then, is the value of psychology? It gives us an understanding of the behavior in question, of a man's thinking and emotions, enabling us to see more clearly how resources of God are to be brought to bear upon a particular emotional problem.

In many instances it is easily seen that the Word of God is superior to the theories of secular psychologists. For example, the Bible gives us a logical basis for self-acceptance: We were created in the image of God and for the purpose of having fellowship with God. We are greatly loved, even in spite of our sinfulness and antagonism toward God (John 3:16; Rom. 5:10). Secular psychology provides no adequate basis for self-acceptance.

In the matter of guilt, secular psychologists have nothing to compare with the divine message of forgiveness of sins through the sacrifice of Jesus Christ. When it comes to man's reason for existence, psychological theories cannot equal the divine purpose for man as set forth in the Bible. And what can the secular psychologist recommend as to human motivation that can supersede the Christian's motivation to glorify God?

It is rather striking to note that every one of the therapeutic approaches recommended in chapter 8 (which were selected primarily because of their effectiveness) can be based squarely upon Scripture. There can be absolutely no doubt about the adequacy of the Word of God and the Spirit of God in meeting those psychological needs that do not have their origin in the physiological.

Is there a danger that the counselor will apply Scriptural and psychological principles in a fleshly manner? A Christian counselor counsels in the flesh when he depends solely upon his ability to diagnose and upon his knowledge of Scriptural therapeutic elements. He counsels in the flesh when he forgets that psychological problems comprise a very large part of a believer's spiritual warfare (Eph. 6:12). And he counsels in the flesh when he does not use spiritual weapons to combat powerful evil forces.

Counseling may be done in the flesh just as witnessing is sometimes done in the flesh when one has an overdependence upon his knowledge of the Scriptures, his ability to meet all objections and his persuasiveness.

A pastor-counselor must be ever mindful of his utter dependence upon prayer, the ministry of the Holy Spirit and the power of the Word of God.

If the counselor gets caught up in his own techniques and fails to use the therapeutic approaches found in Scripture, he may end up helping an unconverted person "sweep his house clean" but still have the problems of the unconverted. He may also lead Christians into an unwarranted confidence in self rather than pointing them to the Lord Jesus Christ Who said, "Without me ye can do nothing."

Because it is so easy for the humanism of secular psychotherapy to creep into a Christian counselor's methodology, he must guard against those temptations to counsel in the flesh by relying much upon prayer and the Word of God.

What is to be the pastor's ultimate authority in the testing of psychological theories? One of the believer's greatest temptations has always been to conform to the world in its thinking. We need to especially guard against this temptation in regard to psychology. The history of Christianity shows that often the Christian has tried to accommodate Biblical teachings to the philosophies and scientific theories of men. The result has been great harm to the cause of Christ. Perhaps in no other field does the Christian find this temptation to accommodate his thinking greater than in the field of psychology. Therefore, no field of study involves greater danger for the believer.

The basic assumptions of a therapist influence his diagnosing, his goals and his methods. How important it is, then, that all assumptions are discovered and compared to the infallible Word of God, the pastor's ultimate authority.

The Bible is the believer's ultimate authority in every area of thought to which it speaks (Isa. 8:20), and it is especially important that we yield to this authority regarding the issues with which psychology is concerned.

Comparisons

This book will compare some of the therapies that are greatly influencing present-day pastoral counseling, with particular attention given to:

> Freud's Psychoanalysis
> Glasser's Reality Therapy
> Drakeford's Integrity Therapy
> Adams's Nouthetic Counseling
> Ellis/Maultsby's Rational Behavior Therapy

The comparison of these psychotherapies will not be limited to one chapter but will be found throughout this work wherever the differences between them are significant.

An overview

This investigation will not involve an in-depth study of the issues treated. Many of them would in themselves provide sufficient material for a book. However, I believe that an overview of this subject matter is greatly needed for those contemplating deeper involvement in a counseling ministry.

To encourage pastors toward deeper involvement in counseling, this book offers a systematic, Scriptural and comprehensive but concise treatment of the basic issues of counseling.

2 The Case for Pastoral Counseling

There is much questioning and discussing among pastors as to whether or not they should become more deeply involved in a counseling ministry. It is therefore imperative that we begin with a definition of pastoral counseling.

Pastoral counseling defined

There are three New Testament words that refer to the pastor: *poimen* (shepherd), *presbuteros* (elder) and *episkopos* (overseer). A pastor is a mature Christian who has been placed as a spiritual leader over a local flock of God by the Holy Spirit (Acts 20:28). His appointment or election by men is a recognition of his divine appointment. His responsibilities include evangelizing (2 Tim. 4:5), leading by example (1 Pet. 5:3), teaching, admonishing, rebuking, warning, training, edifying and restoring. His primary means for accomplishing these objectives is the preaching and teaching of the Word of God (2 Tim. 4:2) in the power of the Spirit of God.

Personal soul winning, then, is one form of pastoral counseling. Soul winning involves a careful presentation of the truth the unconverted person needs to know and believe to be saved. It may also include warning, rebuking, admonishing and beseeching. Almost every soul-winning pastor has seen people dramatically relieved of emotional stress as the direct result of their coming to repentance and faith in the Lord Jesus Christ. But the designation "pastoral counseling" has been limited primarily to the pastoral use of the Word of God in restoring sick or distressed members of the flock of God.

Harold J. Haas prefers to use the designation "counseling" where (1) two persons have knowingly entered into a relationship (2) in which one attempts to help the other and (3) where an established series of meetings is arranged for this purpose.[1] He goes on to say, "Pastoral counseling involves a decision to deal with an individual to alleviate his distress in a particular way."[2] All counseling, according to Haas, is an attempt "to help the person think differently and feel differently about a whole area or several areas of his life."[3]

Psychotherapy is sometimes distinguished from counseling:

> Psychotherapy then usually refers to talking treatment that aims to dig deeply into the person's personality structure to find the cause of mental disorder and to make major changes in the personality to improve the person's situation. . . counseling then refers to treatment that attempts to help a person solve only one or a few specific problems . . . The counseling focuses on *problem situations* rather than major personality reorganization.[4]

Haas's distinctions between pastoral care, pastoral counseling and psychotherapy seem to be artificial and without Scriptural justification. They clearly imply that the Word of God is capable of solving only surface problems and that major personality changes require humanistic methods.

For this reason, it is preferable to define pastoral counseling as any pastoral use of the Word of God along with any other wise counsel for the purpose of changing a person's thinking, feelings or actions to help them realize in their own experience the abundant life that Christ promised.

Pastoral ambivalence

There is much ambivalence among pastors in relation to counseling; they believe counseling is part of their responsibility, but at the same time they find many excuses for not taking that responsibility.

Some are troubled with thoughts of incompetency when they face the strange theories and vocabulary of psychology and the great variety of psychotherapies. They wonder whether or not they could master the subject of counseling sufficiently to be of any practical use.

It is my opinion that a pastor does not need to be an expert in every area of psychology in order to be an effective counselor. A moderate amount of training can give him an adequate grasp of such subjects as human motivations, defense mechanisms, uncovering techniques and therapeutic approaches. He should already be an expert in the use of God's Word, which is the greatest of therapeutic agents. Consultation with Christian men who are trained in psychology or psychiatry will serve to keep him from holding non-Christian psychological positions.

Some pastors are concerned that a greater counseling ministry might take too much time from their already busy schedules. But consider the ministry of our Lord Jesus Christ and the concern that He had for the spiritual, physical, material and emotional welfare of people. We should be willing to examine our own priorities to see if we could eliminate some things to give us the time we need for counseling.

A pastor may also be concerned that, when touching upon a particular issue in a sermon, a counselee will presume that reference is being made to him. This is, of course, one of the occupational hazards of being a pastor. Whenever he preaches God's Word, someone is likely to be convicted or offended. However, a pastor can lessen the possibility that things will be taken personally if he consistently manifests a heart of love, humility and compassion toward those about whom he knows the worst.

There is still the possibility that a counselee will feel uncomfortable knowing that the pastor knows about the darker side of his life; he may move to another church just to escape the embarrassment. In order to avoid jeopardizing his relationship with such individuals, the pastor may choose, when he begins to become aware of an embarrassing issue, to refer such cases to another Christian counselor.

Arguments for pastoral counseling

While acknowledging the few negative aspects of pastoral counseling, it is important that we also acknowledge the many strong arguments in favor of it.

<u>Psychology: a legitimate study.</u> It is just as legitimate for us to study the function of the mind as it is for us to study the function of the body. In fact it seems more appropriate and advantageous for a pastor to study psychology because in regard to soul or mind he is supposed to be an expert. There can be no doubt that emotional problems are usually spiritual problems or have a spiritual dimension.

Throughout the history of Christianity, pastors and spiritual leaders have sought to understand the workings of troubled minds in order to more skillfully apply the Word of God as a means of relief. Some were more gifted and successful than others. And some who engaged in this kind of ministry improved their skills through training and experience.

<u>Pastors are the major source of counseling.</u> The pastor is often the first, and sometimes the only, professional person to whom people go for comfort and counsel when they are in distress. Professor Gary Collins says:

> Several years ago a government-sponsored study discovered that when people had personal problems only 28% of them went to professional counselors or clinics. Approximately 29% consulted their family physician and 42% sought help from clergymen.[5]

These statistics indicate that those who are in distress believe that somehow their problems are related to spiritual and moral issues.

Paul A. Hauck suggests that one of the reasons most distressed people turn to the pastor is because to do so is more face-saving than turning to a psychotherapist (others may consider you sick, neurotic or crazy). "Thus placed in a position that the professional therapist can only envy," Hauck says, "the minister has the kind of ready made atmosphere for counseling that other disciplines must often engineer."[6]

<u>Christian maturity is basic to evangelism.</u> Emotionally ill

saints do not win many souls. Depressed and defeated Christians are likely to provoke the unconverted to say, "If that is what Christianity is, I don't want it." A pastor who is concerned about soul winning must also be concerned about edifying the saints so that they will be qualified to help him in his outreach ministry.

<u>Great emotional needs do exist among Christians.</u> **Probably every emotion experienced by the unconverted is also experienced by God's people.** The Word of God is full of counsel about such things as anxiety, depression, fear, jealousy, anger, frustration and resentment. In almost every instance these emotions involve sinful or irrational thinking. For example:

1. The worried, anxious or fearful person is usually committing the sin of unbelief, that is, he does not trust God's love or His Word.

2. The depressed believer feels rejected, unloved, inadequate and worthless even though his feelings are not well founded on facts. A person's self-concept results not only from the reflected appraisal of significant others, but also from his *interpretation* of this appraisal, which may be greatly perverted through either the devil's insinuations or the individual's own sinful nature.

3. The jealous believer is usually troubled with feelings of insecurity or inadequacy.

4. Believers are sometimes angry because they selfishly and irrationally believe that everything ought to go the way they wish it to go. When their wills are crossed or their plans thwarted they become angry. Research reveals that much anger is related to a *perceived* attack upon one's self-esteem.

It is also believed that emotional factors are involved in many other sins that believers commit. Pride, for example, often masks an underlying low self-concept. The feeling of being a "nobody" has stimulated persons to strive to become "somebody." A critical tongue is often the manifestation of low self-esteem: the critical person is often trying to make himself look better by making others look worse. Sexual promiscuity may result from too little love and needs unmet early in life. Such people are characterized by their striving for immediate gratification. Anger and hostility are quite common in people who are resentful about not having been loved or about missing out on things normally enjoyed by others. The selfish believer is continually discontented and moody and often depressed. He is concerned primarily with his needs, his popularity and his pleasures. Every individual is born with a selfish nature, and he is also placed in a state of helplessness where he must depend upon others to get his needs met. If those needs are not met in the early years of life, much of his later life will be spent in selfish striving for contentment. Such a believer is likely to be carnal or worldly or both. He does not live as unto Christ, Who died for him, or so as to be an encouragement and blessing to others, but as unto himself.

<u>Emotional stress is on the increase in American society.</u> Cardiologists Friedman and Rosenman in their book *Type A Behavior and Your Heart* have pointed out several societal factors that are having a profound impact upon the emotions of men in this present age. Other personal observations have been added to these.

The materialistic outlook of modern Americans. The cardiologists warn, "There is an unbridled drive to acquire more and more of the world's material benefits."[7] They quote Tocqueville as saying, "He who has set his heart upon the pursuit of worldly welfare is always in a hurry for he has but a limited time at his disposal to reach it, to grasp it, and to enjoy it."[8]

The believer is not automatically immune to this hurriedness connected with materialism but is likely to become somewhat caught up in the race.

Our infatuation with speed. The cardiologists ask, "Isn't there truth in the idea that the faster the machine is made to operate, the faster the operator feels he must think and act?"[9]

Our work is governed by production figures and our lives controlled by the clock. We are always racing against deadlines.

The urbanization of society. Living, working and traveling closely with others results in constant frustrations because of the necessity of always being concerned about others' rights, demands and wishes.

America's open economy. In the older societies built upon the class system, or in the newer socialistic society, people have been relieved of the need to struggle for precedence. The pressures of competing in American society have resulted in both physical and emotional stress. In today's society "it is performance, not pedigree that achieves high economic status."[10] This same spirit of competition is found not only among carnal and worldly church members but also among pastors. It is probable that some pastors have died of heart attacks not because they were burning themselves out for God, but because they were driven by the spirit of competition.

Our tendency to reduce men to numbers. This characteristic of our age tends to make people "forget their individual identity and the emotional lineages that draw them together."[11] The resulting feeling of "aloneness" has reinforced man's ordinary and underlying predisposition toward anxiety. In previous times people were more inclined to believe that a watchful God was interested in them personally. They also felt an emotional unity with people who thought as they did.

Proliferation of labor-saving devices. Most physicians and psychiatrists agree that emotional tensions and stress can sometimes be relieved by physical exercise or labor. Our modern labor-saving devices probably keep us from working off our normal tensions.

Working wives and mothers. This trend has resulted in the emotional deprivation of many children and in an increase of unfaithfulness and divorce. Each has devastating emotional consequences.

Religious apostasy. Doubt or denial of the God of the Bible has serious emotional consequences. Such unbelief is likely to result in a sense of being alone in a hostile world. It also leads logically to an emphasis upon the here and now. And since the pleasures of this life cannot satisfy the deepest longings of the human heart, there is likely to be an increase of discontent.

Moral relativism has increased the incidence of guilt. Liberal theology, secular philosophy and humanistic psychology have joined together in promoting a moral relativism. But the personal freedom that it promised has brought many under a great burden of guilt. The increased incidence of sexual looseness and abortions has greatly increased the number of people seeking counseling because of guilt feelings.

An epidemic of inferiority. Some mental health professionals believe they are seeing an epidemic of inferiority in our country. They point out that our society seems to grant respect to only the select few who are considered to meet its standards of beauty, intelligence and unusual skill such as athletic skill. All others are left to cope with feelings of inferiority.

Dobson is convinced that "much of the rebellion, discontent and hostility of the teen-age years emanates from overwhelming uncontrollable feelings of inferiority and inadequacy which rarely find verbal expression."[12] Without a sense of personal worth, both the individual and society suffer.

A transient population. The average American family moves once every five years. Children grow up having no roots; there is no place that they can really call home. The resulting lack of a sense of belonging tends to remove some of the restraints upon behavior and lessens the number of people who really care about the individual when he is in trouble.

The influence of deterministic psychology. The deterministic psychoanalysis of Freud has held sway in psychotherapy up to the present time, although its influence is being diminished somewhat by contemporary existentialist psychologies. The existentialists believe that within the limitations of one's constitution, it is possible for him to choose future programs of action.

Martin Gross writes:

Sigmund Freud and the environmentalists who succeeded him have changed that. In their psychological child care system which has infiltrated millions of psyches world-wide, the child is a tender, vulnerable reed very susceptible to parents' influence. In this system, *it is the parents, not the child, who are tested.* If they have done a good job, it will be seen in the actions and stability of the child. In one graceful psychological move, responsibility has shifted from emerging person to parent, from *self to others.* [Italics in the original.][13]

And Gross further states, "Not unlike the parent who once feared a summertime polio attack, the contemporary parent is constantly anxious about the child's precarious emotional state."[14] Besides suffering anxiety, the parents also bear a heavy load of guilt if the child does not live up to society's expectations of him.

The Freudians, who accuse religious leaders of heaping guilt upon society, have themselves been responsible for making parents feel guilty for not providing the right environment for their troubled children.

<u>Pastors must not abdicate their responsibility.</u> Pastors have a God-given responsibility to teach, warn, rebuke and admonish the sheep of their flocks (Col. 3:16; 2 Tim. 4:2). The word *nouthesia* (admonition) upon which Jay Adams bases his Nouthetic Counseling,[15] signifies "putting people in mind" of the truths that they specifically need at a particular time. Since emotional distress cannot help influencing one's worship, spiritual outlook, measure of victory over sin and the effectiveness of his service and witness, it seems imperative that the pastor be involved when his people have emotional problems.

Those pastors who, like this writer, are convinced that sinful or irrational thinking is at the root of most painful emotions and unacceptable behavior will surely recognize and accept the responsibility for seeking to bring the thinking of their people into conformity with the Word of God.

It would also seem obligatory for pastors to help their people avoid the dangers of walking "in the counsel of the ungodly" (Ps. 1:1). Any psychotherapist who claims to leave religion entirely out of his counseling is not being honest. Almost all psychotherapy of whatever method deals with such things as religious beliefs, morals, goals, the meaning of life, sin and guilt. And most psychotherapists, either directly or indirectly, aim for changes in the thinking of their counselees. Whether they admit it or not, they are transmitting their values.

In all fairness we must admit that some, like Albert Ellis,

clearly state that changing minds is a major aim of their therapy. Ellis tells us that his goal is:

> To subtly or honestly induce subjects to change their beliefs, attitudes, opinions or philosophies . . . they will at the same time almost automatically make significant and often highly dramatic changes in their emotions and behavior.[16]

Martin Gross quotes Hiram K. Johnson as saying:

> It is impossible to overemphasize the fact that the direct implications of the concepts and methods of psychoanalysis inevitably lead the researcher into the area of theology.[17]

Monte H. Liebman tells us:

> We recognize, in part, that the therapeutic process is a decoding and recoding of the person's life code, and like any unscrambling process, it is more efficiently accomplished if there is less distraction and interference by other people's systems. I think this fact is not appreciated enough.[18]

The many anti-Christian statements of Freud would confirm that psychoanalysis and Christianity do not agree concerning some very crucial issues such as personal responsibility, guilt and the cure of emotional problems.

Even though the secular psychologist does not seek to contradict or destroy his counselee's religious faith, he still could do spiritual harm to a believer, and he certainly would be at a handicap in dealing with a believer's problems. The pastor, working in a Christian context, will be able to understand the religious and ethical aspects of this person's problems in a way that the secularist never can.

In light of these facts, how can a conscientious and godly pastor refuse to do the work of counseling his flock?

<u>Pastors generally have personal and professional qualifications necessary for counseling.</u> Those pastors who are truly born-again also have the wisdom of the Spirit of God, and generally are well taught in the Word of God.

The Spirit-filled, Bible-taught pastor needs to recognize the qualifications and value the resources he has to help him meet emotional needs. Should not such pastors prayerfully consider spending the necessary time and effort to learn better how the human mind functions?

3 Qualifications for Pastoral Counseling

A brochure advertising a program for training salesmen stated that most prospects "buy" the salesman who calls on them as much as they buy the product or service he offers. There is a great deal of agreement among psychotherapists of almost every school that a similar relationship exists between counselor and counselee. Few people are helped by a counselor they can not *buy* as a person. Somehow the counselor must communicate not only his personality, values, attitudes and beliefs to the counselee, but also something of his knowledge and skill in helping emotionally distressed people. In the Christian realm, this must be the work of the Holy Spirit. There are two categories of qualifications that are vital in pastoral counseling—personal and professional.

Personal qualifications

The personality of the counselor is the most decisive factor in the process of psychotherapy. "A minister's personality," Clinebell says, "is his only instrument for communicating the Good News through relationships."[1]

Dean Johnson is quoted by Clinebell as saying:

Counseling is not merely the use of certain techniques. It is first of all the counselor's use of himself in a manner that helps the counselee to do something constructive about his trouble. The key is not so much the techniques employed, important as they are, as it is the total attitude of the counselor, how he feels about people, what he believes about them and about himself.[2]

When the counselee perceives certain characteristics in the counselor, by the way he responds during counseling to what the counselee says and does, the counselee begins to change and grow as a person. Since psychotherapy brings help through interpersonal relationships and the personal attitude of the counselee toward the counselor is of such importance, great care must be given to elicit a positive response from the counselee. This emphasis upon the personality of the counselor is a great departure from the socially distant analyst of Freudian psychoanalysis.

The following are some of the important personal qualifications for pastoral counseling:

<u>Regenerate.</u> The testimonies of several pastors whom I have known personally make it clear that a man may be a pastor and yet unregenerate. Unless a man is regenerated by the Spirit of God, it is not likely that he will understand as fully as the believer either the cause or the cure of emotional distress. Paul tells us, "The natural man receiveth not the things of the Spirit of God: for they are foolishness unto him: neither can he know them, because they are spiritually discerned" (1 Cor. 2:14).

Only a regenerate pastor can have the leading of the Holy Spirit in the application of Scriptural truth to the hearts of needy people. The converted pastor also has the privilege of prayer and the promise that he will be given the wisdom of God in ministering to troubled hearts (James 1:5).

<u>Spiritual.</u> Paul indicates that the ministry of restoring those who have been overtaken in faults belongs to those who are "spiritual" (Gal. 6:1). A spiritual Christian is one whose life is characterized by the control of the Holy Spirit rather than the control of his fleshly nature. His life will be full of goodness (Rom. 15:14). He is in regular communion with God through prayer and the reading of Scripture. His first concern is the Kingdom of God, not his own interests. A spiritual Christian is one who has a genuine concern for the well-being of the Lord's people and of people in general. Jesus indicated to Peter that if he loved Him, he

would feed His sheep (John 21:15–17).

<u>Gentle.</u> Paul admonishes us to restore a troubled brother in a spirit of meekness [gentleness] (Gal.6:1). He will be gentle because he realizes that he too could be tempted and fall. Instead of condemning he will be forgiving. He will say, "There go I but for the grace of God."

Clinebell says:

> To recognize that the regressed catatonic on the back ward of the mental hospital is more like than different from oneself shakes to the very foundation of our defensive self-image. To accept this truth at a deep level is possible for most of us only to a limited degree. It requires an inward surrender of subtle feelings of self-idolatry and spiritual superiority.[3]

The counselor's awareness of his own fallibility is bound to be conveyed to the counselee and will render the counselee more receptive to his efforts.

Gentleness will tend to curb the counselor's coercive or manipulative tendencies. He will patiently await the preparatory work of the Holy Spirit before urging upon the counselee some difficult course of action. It will also prevent the counselor from being cruel and inconsiderate. Before telling the counselee what he needs to know, the counselor will seek to make sure that he has sufficient ego strength to bear it.

<u>Genuine.</u> Genuineness means being freely, deeply and genuinely oneself. An effective counselor must be open and honest about himself, he must be real and transparent, avoiding all role-playing, phoniness or hypocrisy. His words must be consistent with his actions. And if what a counselor says and does becomes removed from his real feelings and attitudes, the counselee will sense it and judge it as "putting on," and the counselor will therefore lose his effectiveness.

Haas points out the peculiarity of the pastor's problem in this regard:

> The problem is even more complex for the pastor, more so than

for the psychologist or psychiatrist, because as a Christian the pastor *is* committed to filling a role that is contrary to his nature. He is committed to living the Good Life, the moral life, when by nature he is, like all other men, self-centered and sinful.

Most mental health professionals are only committed to living like decent human beings. And technically they are only committed to being decent human beings during office hours. In contrast the pastor has taken on, and he has had ascribed to him by others, the role of an exemplar of the faith.[4]

The counselee needs to know that the pastor is willing to admit his own temptations and failures; that he is a redeemed sinner daily needing the grace of God.

The truly genuine counselor will be spontaneous but not impulsive or disrespectful. A genuine concern will cause him to guard against needlessly sharing any negative feelings he may have toward the counselee.

<u>Warm.</u> Basil Jackson has pointed out that the counselor's personal warmth or propensity to bestow love is related to his own maturity. He says:

> Maturity is also related to the capacity to relate intimately with other human individuals without doing violence to their inner dignity and autonomy. This includes the ability and willingness to be compassionate toward all men, while at the same time expressing a respectful understanding and appreciation of the human condition per se and demonstrating a propensity to bestow love rather than to await its reception.[5]

Warmth, caring and loving are shown by a smile, tone of voice, gestures, posture and direct eye contact. It may also be manifested by being available at all times, even at the cost of having plans interrupted. Such warmth or love does not need to be talked about; it is as evident as the warmth from a stove.

The effectiveness of personal warmth and love is illustrated by the work of John Rosen, the founder of the concept of "direct psychoanalysis." Alphonse Calabrese, a New York City psychiatrist who had recently accepted Christ as Savior, tells what a great impact Dr. Rosen's keynote speech at the American Academy of Psychotherapists made on him. Speaking of Dr. Rosen, he says:

> His pioneering efforts in the field were legendary. While working at a New York hospital, he decided that the usual methods of treating the hopeless schizophrenics, including shock therapy and isolated hospitalization, were archaic and primitive. He believed that the best way to deal with these people was to show them love and to become, in effect, a real mother to them. He began to feed, bathe and dress the hopelessly insane patients, and he would read children's stories to them and tuck them into bed.
>
> Authorities at the hospital told him either to follow the philosophy of the staff administration or to leave, so he complied with their rules during the daytime. But at night he slipped into the wards and continued to care for these patients with the compassionate approach he was developing. His tremendous success catapulted him to a leading position in the field and he became the leader of the new school of thought, which was dubbed "direct psychoanalysis."[6]

Dr. Rosen concluded his speech by saying, "I do know if we are to reach the people we work with, we psychotherapists have to become more Christ-like."[7]

The experience of psychotherapists seems to confirm that people grow by being known and loved. They have also discovered that people grow defectively and fail to mature in an atmosphere of inattention or denigration.

When a counselor likes and pays attention to a counselee, the counselee comes to think of himself as better, more worthwhile and less helpless than he had been thinking; he begins to gain self-esteem by his intimate association with one who generally has a high self-concept.

Nathaniel Branden warns against taking Carl Rogers's "unconditional positive regard" too literally. He says:

> To have *"unconditional* positive regard" means: to value him whether or not one finds anything in him to value, to value him whether or not any of his distinctive qualities are positively mean-

ingful to oneself. To have "unconditional positive regard" for him means to experience him as a value to oneself regardless of anything he is or does. If such an attitude were possible, which it is not, it would give the client an appallingly unrealistic view of the nature of human relationships; it would not be helpful but harmful.[8]

From a natural viewpoint Branden's argument seems to hold up against Rogers's view. But the Christian who has the Holy Spirit motivating him is enabled to love the unlovable and to see even a depraved and despicable individual as one for whom Christ died and whom He can make into a new creature.

<u>Empathetic.</u> Harper clearly sets forth Rogers's views concerning empathy:

> The therapist must experience an empathic understanding of the client's awareness of his own experience and he must try to communicate this empathic understanding to the client. The definition Rogers gives of empathic understanding is that of sensing the client's internal frame of reference as if it were his (the therapist's) own without the therapist losing his own separate emotional existence. It is the ability of the therapist to sense the client's emotions without himself getting emotionally tied up with them.[9]

In illustrating empathy or "feeling into," Collins uses an experience most of us have had when riding in a car as a passenger. When seeing the need to slow down, we have pushed our foot on the floor. We were feeling into the driver's situation.[10]

The counselor enters into the inner world of the counselee through listening with awareness. The counselor asks himself, "If I were in his situation, how would I feel?" Empathy is understanding the other person from his own point of view and feeling some of what the other person is feeling. It is "crawling into the other person's world."[11]

The pastor who is likely to have a large degree of empathy is the one who has suffered much himself. Paul says, "Blessed be God, even the Father of our Lord Jesus Christ, the Father of mercies, and the God of all comfort; Who comforteth us in all our tribulation, that we may be able to comfort them which are in any trouble, by the comfort wherewith we ourselves are comforted of God" (2 Cor. 1:3, 4).

<u>Self-knowledgeable.</u> The pastor cannot help others if he does not know himself well enough to help himself. The pastor's self-awareness encourages the same process in the counselee.

Self-knowledge is the ability to realistically evaluate oneself. It is understanding one's own mental processes, reactions and abilities.[12] It is being open and honest with your emotional problems. Basil Jackson tells of the importance of accurate self-knowledge:

> Reluctance or complete inability to look at one's self in an insightful way also has clear spiritual correlates. The Bible clearly points out that the self in its natural and unregenerate condition is not a thing of beauty. Jesus took pains to elucidate this in detail when He described the negative potentialities of the human heart or psyche (Mark 7:15, 21). Many of the individuals this author sees clinically, who come from certain segments of the evangelical community, at times do all in their power to ignore and repress the presence of basic aggressive and sexual forces within them. Such a failure to appraise realistically what is within one's self can produce various types of maladaptations or neuroses, which unfortunately often come to be considered concrete evidence of sanctification. The logical progression of this type of thinking is a change from mere repression to complete denial which may eventuate in a typical "holiness" theology. Without insight, mere repression may be construed as holiness.[13]

One of the barriers to self-awareness, according to Clinebell, is self-centeredness. He says, "self-centeredness and depth self-awareness are opposite psychological conditions. The self-centered person is aware mainly of his own painful insecurity and demanding need for attention."[14]

How often, then, must we as pastor-counselors ask the Lord to search our hearts and see if there be any wicked way in us (Ps. 139:23, 24).

<u>Spiritually mature.</u> The counselor should not be a novice but one who knows well his own sinful tendencies and the means

of spiritual warfare. He must know the power of the cross and of the Holy Spirit to deal with the flesh. He must know how to appropriate the resurrection life of Christ.

<u>Wise.</u> Wisdom is a gift from God (1 Cor. 12:8). It may be implied from 1 Thessalonians 5:12 (". . . know them which labor among you, and are over you in the Lord, and admonish you") that every divinely-called pastor has been given, to some degree, the gift of wisdom so as to admonish his flock. He is expected to be able to form rational judgments and to give godly counsel. He is expected to have skill in the application of general Biblical principles to particular problem situations. "Preach the word; be instant in season, out of season; reprove, rebuke, exhort with all longsuffering and doctrine" (2 Tim. 4:2).

Wisdom includes the ability to establish a good rapport with people of different backgrounds and to communicate well with them as both listener and speaker.

Without this gift of wisdom a man is not likely to be a competent counselor even though he may have had training in both theology and psychology. How does a man know that he possesses this gift? It seems that the best answer is in the one word *success.* If he possesses the gift of wisdom he is likely to have some success in counseling. Believers as well as nonbelievers will observe his success and will begin to seek him out for counsel.

Wolpe is quoted by Harper as saying:

> The patient often has positive emotional responses as he confidentially reveals and talks about his difficulties to a person he believes to be knowledgeable, skillful and desirous of helping him. If these emotional responses which tend to be antagonistic to anxiety are of sufficient strength, they will reciprocally inhibit the anxiety responses that are evoked by some of the subject matter of the interview. Therapeutic effects will thus occur.[15]

Without some evidence of possessing this gift of wisdom, a ministry of counseling will produce nothing but frustration and failure.

<u>Trustworthy.</u> Since the counselor's relationship with the

counselee is a vital aspect of counseling, it is of utmost importance that there be an attitude of **trust** and confidence toward the counselor. It can rightly be said that trust is the basis of the relationship.

When people relate their deepest feelings, a counselor must be very careful with the trust—that is, careful not to divulge those feelings. Nothing can be so destructive of a counseling relationship as a counselee learning from someone else what he has spoken in private.

When a strong sense of confidence develops toward the counselor, the person opens up himself more fully and can therefore be better enabled to solve his problems.

<u>Optimistic.</u> One of the most helpful things a pastor can communicate to his counselee is a sense of **hope.** Without hope, the counselee is likely to soon break off the relationship.

The truly born-again pastor has a powerful element in his counseling that the unconverted counselor cannot possibly emulate: the pastor cannot help communicating what he believes. If he truly believes the Bible to be the infallible Word of God, its teachings and principles will be much more effectively applied. If he truly believes that Jesus Christ conquered death by His resurrection, it will be evident when he ministers to the person who is facing death from an incurable disease. When the pastor believes in the resurrection of the saints and the return of the Lord Jesus Christ, it will make a difference when he is counseling those who have recently lost a loved one through death. Many times I have been surprised to find clergymen afraid to even speak of death. Some of them find it very difficult to visit with those who are not expected to live.

The pastor who believes in the superabounding grace of God will evidence hope for even the vilest of sinners. Those who have personally experienced God's transforming power will have no doubt about God's ability to change someone else. Those who have experienced the abundant life Jesus Christ promised will manifest an enthusiasm for life that many secular counselors cannot.

The pastor who believes that the Holy Spirit wants to counsel and guide believers will often pray with his counselees for the wisdom of God.

Professional qualifications

Training in theology and Scripture is vital if one believes that facing reality is important to emotional maturity. Since God's Word is truth, no man can face reality until he has faced the most basic realities of life set forth in the Scriptures: man's origin, his sinful nature, his reason for existence, divinely established values, man's accountability, his possibility of redemption and his destiny.

Colossians 3:16 seems to indicate that letting the Word of Christ dwell richly in us, in all wisdom, is a prerequisite to "teaching and admonishing one another."

<u>Training in psychology.</u> The study of the human mind is as justified for the pastor as studying the human body is for the physician. Therefore, a pastor should seek to know as much as he can about the functioning of the human mind with which he is constantly dealing. He should seek to understand human needs and motivation, the nature of emotions, causes of emotional distress, defense mechanisms and uncovering techniques.

Charles Solomon says:

> Rare, indeed, is the individual who employs psychology exclusively for the purpose of understanding the psycho-dynamics of the behavior in question, while allowing the Spirit of God to apply the Word of God to produce a child of God and that child of God being "conformed to His image" (see Rom. 8:29).[16]

It is true that the vast amount of literature and the great degree of disagreement found in it at first makes such an investigation seem overwhelming. But a pastor may save much time by having his reading guided by those who are soundly trained in both theology and psychology.

The psychological training needed by the pastor-counselor will be determined by the kind of counseling he employs. Short-term uncovering or Nouthetic Counseling will not require a great deal of psychological training. A pastor seeking to do "insight counseling" will certainly have to be trained more extensively in the matters referred to previously (human needs and motivation, the nature of emotions, etc.).

The question arises, If the counselor does not have insight into the counselee's "real" problem, how can he be realistic and effective in the use of Scripture to meet that problem?

It seems to me that a pastor needs to know how to practice "insight counseling" to the extent that he will be able to help in the "average" case of neurosis. He should also be able to ascertain when the counselee needs to be referred to a competent Christian psychiatrist because of psychosis, a difficult case of neurosis such as obsession-compulsion or when there is a massive reservoir of feeling that cannot be controlled by thinking.

The importance of the counselor's personality, spirituality and gifts to the progress of counseling seems to indicate that his personal qualifications may be an indication of his calling. Those who believe they have the gifts and calling of God for pastoring and counseling should obtain the psychological training commensurate with the degree of their involvement in counseling and with the claims of other priorities.

4 Theological Presuppositions in Pastoral Counseling

The Bible-believing pastor has a responsibility to make certain that his counseling is either directly based upon Scripture or in harmony with it. Otherwise he may find himself using satanic or fleshly methods. He must be careful that what he says in counseling is congruent with what he says in the pulpit.

Because theological implications of the various psychotherapies are not clearly evident, it becomes necessary that we search for them, and upon discovering them test them by our ultimate authority, the Bible.

The following are the theological presuppositions upon which a Scripturally defensible psychotherapy must be based:

The existence of God

There is a God before whom we live and to whom we must give account of ourselves. It may be said that more consequences for thought and action follow the affirmation or denial of God than from answering any other basic question. Some people who could not otherwise be persuaded to do so have quit their sin when they realized that someday they would stand in judgment before a holy God.

Freud's view seems to be that, even if there were a divine judgment, the individual could escape it by blaming his parents and others for his early environment. Glasser insists that the individual must accept responsibility for his actions, but it is a non-Christian responsibility. He says nothing about being responsible before God; his definition of moral behavior does not even hint of God: "When a man acts in such a way that he gives and receives love, and feels worthwhile to himself and others, his behavior is right or moral."[1] Such a definition places morality on the same basis as Joseph Fletcher's situation ethics. Ellis, by his own admission, is also in agreement with Fletcher.[2] Drakeford does not talk of responsibility toward God, probably because he believes that "values arise from the consensus of the society within which we live."[3] It is evident that he accepts the relationship basis of morality as set forth by Kirkendall, whom he quotes as saying:

> Whenever a decision or a choice is to be made concerning behavior, the moral decision will be the one which works toward the creation of trust, confidence, and integrity in relationships. It should increase the capacity of individuals to cooperate, and enhance the sense of self-respect in the individual. Acts which create distrust, suspicion, and misunderstanding, which build barriers and destroy integrity, are immoral. They decrease the individual's sense of self-respect, and rather than producing a capacity to work together they separate people and break down the capacity for communication.[4]

Of the psychotherapies that we are comparing, only Adams's Nouthetic Counseling teaches a clear-cut responsibility toward God.

Nietzsche clearly saw the relationship between the doctrine of God and the limitation of human behavior. "Only when there is no God," he said, "does man become free."[5]

A Bible-believing pastor will be careful not to disregard the anti-God sentiments that are either explicit or implicit in many of the modern psychotherapies. The fact of God is one of the realities, in fact the greatest reality, that an individual must face. When a counselee ignores the reality of God and builds his life around a materialist philosophy, he is not likely to find emotional relief. He is likely, rather, to become driven, restless, bored or despairing. Man's soul can find no rest until it rests in God.

Man was created by God

Man is not the product of accidental and physical forces; he is a creature designed by a personal God. Man was created with both a material and a nonmaterial nature. He is from both dust and God.

Theologians, physiologists and psychologists often find themselves in serious disagreement on this issue. Some theologians hold that human mental activity is not wholly dependent on the physical brain. Those who believe that a believer can experience the presence of his Lord while his body (brain included) is in the grave (Phil. 1:23) are those who hold that physical brain activity does not comprise one hundred percent of mental activity. J.D. Radcliff in his *Reader's Digest* article "I Am Joe's Brain" has the brain saying, "I'm more than a part of him, I *am* Joe—the governor of all his acts, feelings, thoughts and emotions."[6] According to this view, if Joe were to be killed in an explosion, he would cease to exist.

Psychological research on human and animal brains proving the great similarity between them anatomically, biochemically or electrically, does not provide adequate explanation for vast differences in mental activity between them. There seems to be no physical explanation. The element of man that is nonmaterial makes the difference.

Man was created for God's pleasure

Revelation 4:11 reads, "Thou art worthy, O Lord, to receive glory and honour and power: for thou hast created all things, and for thy pleasure they are and were created." Only when man is fulfilling the divine purpose for his existence will he find a deep sense of meaning in his life. According to the Bible, the chief purpose of man is to glorify God (1 Cor. 10:31).

Man was created as a morally responsible being (unlike the animals)

We cannot rationally condemn the boa constrictor that recently was found wrapped tightly around the dead owner's neck.

However, because man by nature has a conscience that either accuses or excuses him for his actions (Rom. 2:14, 15), he is responsible for what he thinks and does.

Man was created in a state of innocency

When man came from the hand of God he was very good (Gen. 1:31). Man's present imperfect and sinful condition is not due to poor workmanship on God's part but rather to human sin.

Man was made in the image of God

"And God said, Let us make man in our image, after our likeness . . ." (Gen. 1:26a). Man's likeness to God is seen primarily in his intellectual ability, his moral and social nature and especially in his spiritual capacity—his capacity for communication with God. Since this is the most unique characteristic of man, it is unlikely that a man can find deep satisfaction apart from having fellowship with God.

When a counselee begins to realize that God originally made man "very good" and in His own image with the capacity for communicating with God, he may begin to see that he is of great importance to God in spite of his sinfulness.

Man became depraved

Bible-believing pastors would not agree with Jess Lair who said, "Everyone who is willing to try finds a power and glory and majesty within them [sic] that is just breathtaking."[7] Neither on the basis of Scripture nor in the realities of life can we conclude that man is innately good or that human progress is inevitable.

By depravity we mean that there is nothing in fallen man that pleases God. Even though men may see good in a person who shows kindness or makes personal sacrifices for others, God sees a heart that is basically antagonistic toward Himself and His law. Man's spiritual state is such that no effort of his will can bring about a radical change of his heart. Therefore, unless God intervenes by grace, man remains in a condition of antagonism toward God. The universality of depravity is seen in Romans 3:10 and 23, where it states that all men, under all circumstances, in every age and under whatever educational influence they may be brought up, begin to sin uniformly as soon as they become old enough to know right from wrong.

There is a great deal of agreement among thinking men that something is seriously wrong with human nature. Einstein stated after World War II that something is desperately wrong with the hearts and minds of men. Freud said, "I have found little that is 'good' about human beings on the whole. In my experience most of them are trash."[8] And Kovel said, "We are inevitably neurotic."[9] Liebman says, "We recognize inherent in the nature of man not flawless being, but corruptible being."[10]

The following are Scriptural indications of human depravity:

<u>Self-centered.</u> The Scripture indicates that men normally "live unto themselves" (2 Cor. 5:15). When Adam and Eve first doubted God, self rather than God became the center of their lives and they began to look out for themselves. This self-centeredness led them to seek to become equal with God. It was the reason for their greedy stealing of the fruit. Man's original love and trust toward God had become transformed "into an unchained, demonic and destructive egoism. . . ."[11] Roberts writes:

> Most of us do strive for security by trying to organize the universe around ourselves. And most of us learn only through the suffering and estrangement which attend egocentricity that this way leads not to security, but to an endlessly precarious and ultimately fruitless attempt to twist reality into meeting our private specifications.[12]

It may be said that selfishness is the basis of every other sin. It is, no doubt, also basic to every mental distress and especially to the deep-seated anxiety that is the lot of every human being. A selfish looking out for oneself, instead of loving and trusting God, cannot help resulting in anxiety, for man has no sure confidence that he can take care of himself. Man cannot be at peace within himself until he becomes God-centered.

<u>A will antagonistic toward God.</u> "The carnal mind is enmity against God: for it is not subject to the law of God, neither indeed can be" (Rom. 8:7). Since Adam, men have not been seeking God but rather have been running away from Him. Even when men clearly know the way God would have them go, they turn to their own way (Isa. 53:6).

<u>Dead toward God.</u> "And you hath he quickened, who were dead in trespasses and sins" (Eph. 2:1). When a person is dead in sin he is dead toward God and has no disposition to love, honor, obey or fellowship with God. His religious works are "dead works" and cannot please God.

<u>A deceitful heart.</u> The Bible tells us, "The heart is deceitful above all things, and desperately wicked . . ." (Jer. 17:9), and "The wicked are estranged from the womb: they go astray as soon as they be born, speaking lies" (Ps. 58:3). One of man's most basic problems is untruthfulness, which results in all kinds of evil. Maultsby believes that man has an unusual ability to distort the truth.[13] Man tends to distort the reality of the outside world and also the truth about his own inner thoughts. Mental illness involves a distortion in the way a person sees himself and other people. He tells himself lies and believes them, then he acts upon them as though they were true. Basil Jackson stated in a lecture, "All psychotherapy is an exercise in telling the truth."[14] Some people are stubbornly unwilling to admit that they have done wrong because they have falsely convinced themselves of their innocence.

<u>A darkened understanding.</u> "But the natural man receiveth not the things of the Spirit of God: for they are foolishness unto him: neither can he know them, because they are spiritually discerned" (1 Cor. 2:14).

"But if our gospel be hid, it is hid to them that are lost: In whom the god of this world hath blinded the minds of them which believe not, lest the light of the glorious gospel of Christ, who is the image of God, should shine unto them" (2 Cor. 4:3, 4).

"Having the understanding darkened, being alienated from the life of God through the ignorance that is in them, because of the blindness of their heart" (Eph. 4:18).

Because the understanding is darkened, man cannot see that his way of thinking is futile. Neither can he see his spiritual needs. Therefore, it is possible for him to hear the gospel clearly presented and still not comprehend it.

An evil imagination (Gen. 6:5). The Hebrew word for "imagination" means "the thing framed." The things fallen man frames in his mind are evil—his imaginations, his intentions and his plans.

A defective conscience. Conscience is the moral nature with which every man is born. It is the light "which lighteth every man" (John 1:9). Because of the fall of Adam, the conscience of every one of his descendants has been dulled so that it does not respond adequately when sin is contemplated or committed. In some, the conscience has been seared (1 Tim. 4:2) so that it is "past feeling" (Eph. 4:19). Early childhood experiences are also a factor in the molding of the conscience.

Because the conscience is so badly abused over a long period of time, it becomes calloused and no longer gives trustworthy moral guidance. In order for it to function at its best, a man's conscience must be informed by both the Spirit of God and the Word of God.

Believing counselors need to be aware of the Freudian view that the conscience is merely the internalized voice of one's parents. Freud's method involved the quieting or changing of the conscience in order to get rid of guilt.

Controlled by Satan. All unregenerate people walk according to "the prince of the power of the air" (Eph. 2:2). The whole world is controlled by the wicked one (1 John 5:19). It is my belief that Satan controls unregenerate man by influencing his thinking. Unregenerate man certainly is not a free moral agent—he is a slave to sin and to Satan and needs to be set free by the Son of God (John 8:36).

A slave to sin. Theologians and psychologists are seriously divided among themselves on the issue of man's autonomy. Some theologians and psychologists view man as self-determined. Others take what I believe to be the Scriptural position—that human behavior is neither fully determined nor fully free.

Concerning this issue, it is ironic that many anti-Freudians find some measure of agreement with Freud, while some followers of Glasser and Drakeford find that they must disagree with them. Perhaps Freud best represents the position of **determinism.** Gross quotes Freud as saying, "The ego is not a master in its own house."[15] Freud's basic theory is that most behavior is predetermined by previous experiences, especially one's experience with his parents. Freud's position has been summarized by Jackson: "What I am today depends upon what I was yesterday."[16]

This view of man reduces selfhood to the level of societal slavery. A man cannot make purposeful changes in the world. He is a product of his environment and nothing else, so he is simply responding to the stimuli of his environment. There are no choices or decisions. This view wipes out any form of accountability, responsibility or freedom.

The position of autonomy or **self-determination** is represented by such writers as Glasser, Branden, Drakeford, Frankl and Ellis. These men reject all the theories that make man a victim of heredity or environment. They all believe that man is able to change his behavior by rational thinking or by making responsible choices. Basil Jackson summarizes Frankl's view as follows: "What I am today is not so much dependent on what I was yesterday but upon what I choose to be today."[17]

Branden, who strongly opposes determinism, states:

This approach stands in rather sharp contrast to that of most contemporary psychologists and psychiatrists, who tend to see man as a passive, helplessly determined product of his environment and genetic inheritance, and who seems singularly indifferent to the fact that man's biologically distinguishing characteristic, and basic means of survival, is his power of conceptual thought—his ability to reason. They evidently have not discovered that a species' distinctive means of survival, of coping with the environment, has the most profound implications for its behavior . . . the most ignored (and usually denied) aspect of the human personality: man's power of self-determination.[18]

Those who hold to this humanistic view believe that man himself is quite able to solve his emotional problems. They would deny the Scriptural teaching of original sin and man's bondage to sin (Rom. 6:17, 18). They do not see man's need of the grace of God to bring about change in his behavior.

The third position, which I believe is the Scriptural one, is that man is neither fully determined nor fully free. Conscious intention can influence events, as seen in our choices of academic courses, toothpaste, wives and politicians. Decision making is a part of our everyday lives. It is just not possible to ignore the seeming freedom of choice and action that is common to men of all cultures and ages. But is the seeming freedom of choice an illusion? What do the Scriptures teach?

The Scriptures abound with references wherein God holds man accountable for his deeds (Rev. 20:13). God never treats man as a puppet but always as a responsible person. The ability of man to choose, at least in most matters, is clearly taught in Scripture. In fact, it is a person's habitual choices that largely determine his character, and character is the determining factor in all behavior. Roberts says, "The character structure being what it is at a given moment, the thoughts, the feelings, and actions of the moment follow necessarily."[19]

Since choices are made from early in life, it is likely that a person will become the prisoner of early irrational decisions. Man's choices determine not only his character but often his environment as well.

A person can commit an act so often that it becomes a habit, and then it becomes his nature. Most of us would agree that one's choosing to smoke his first cigarette is a comparatively free act, but we would not consider the smoking of his three thousandth cigarette a free act. Choices determine character, and man is bound by the chains of his nature.

Again we must face the issue of whether or not those "free" choices or actions were greatly influenced by unconscious motivations. Some believe that, in his unconscious functioning at least, the neurotic's behavior is determined by his past. It is believed that the degree of an individual's freedom is related greatly to the degree of his internal harmony, to his awareness of his total motivation. "The more *conscience* and *impulse* are in conflict with each other, the more compulsive does the expression of both become," says Roberts.[20] But when thoughts, feelings and actions harmonize with each other there is a great feeling of freeness in the action. An individual may be more driven by unconscious motivation at one time than another. Therefore, the degree of an individual's freedom fluctuates constantly.

The impact of one's self-concept upon behavior is clearly taught in such passages as Ephesians 5:3, "But fornication, and all uncleanness, or covetousness, let it not be once named among you, *as becometh saints*"; and in verse 8 we read, "For ye were sometimes darkness, but now *are ye light* in the Lord: walk as children of light."

The effects of bad environment upon behavior are taught all through Scripture. The Israelites were to keep themselves separate from the pagan peoples of Canaan. The Christians were warned by Paul, "Be not deceived: evil communications corrupt good manners" (1 Cor. 15:33). The Scriptures teach, then, that social environment does greatly influence one's behavior but does not determine it.

The fact that men are born with a fleshly nature (John 3:6) and that it is antagonistic toward God and cannot please God (Rom. 8:7, 8) is clear Scriptural evidence that man apart from the grace of God is not free to either choose God or please Him. Jesus Christ clearly said, ". . . Whosoever committeth sin is the servant of sin" (John 8:34).

Behavior is also influenced by the Spirit of God. When a person is regenerated by accepting Christ and receiving the Holy Spirit, he becomes a new creature; his life is transformed. And the believer who submits to the control of the Holy Spirit experiences a life that is characterized by victory over the fleshly nature (Gal. 5:16).

Sin nature: the basic cause of emotional distress

Man's sinful nature is the basic cause of most emotional and mental distress. Some mental distress is caused by genetic or physiological factors, but most mental distress is the result of sinful attitudes and self-deceit. People make their own problems. If all mental distress is caused by disease, then a man is not responsible for his actions. Instead of going to jail for antisocial behavior, he should be sent to a hospital. And if disease is the problem, why should people talk to a psychiatrist? No one has ever talked a person out of a disease.

Clinebell, Glasser, Drakeford, Ellis and Adams would all subscribe to the view that counselors should follow the educational model rather than the medical model. Counselees need instruction, not medicine, because they are emotionally ill, not physically ill.

Clinebell's "revised model" regards "creative teaching methods as indispensable to much pastoral counseling."[21]

God loves sinners

God loves sinners while they are yet morally helpless, sinning, and even indifferent and antagonistic toward Him (Rom. 5:8, 10). The great love of God toward sinners is perhaps best illustrated by His love for Saul of Tarsus, the "chiefest" of sinners (1 Tim. 1:15). God's love for the sinner is such that it expressed itself in sacrificial action: The Father sent His Son into the world and to the cruel cross for us, and the Son came willingly to bear mockery, reproach and a shameful and cruel death for us.

It is because of God's undeserved love for sinners that the self-depreciating and emotionally distressed person may find the basis for a renewed self-concept. Christ promises those who come to Him that He will for no reason refuse them (John 6:37). By His love, God calls us His sons (1 John 3:1) and He makes us heirs of God and joint heirs with Jesus Christ (Rom. 8:17).

God does not tell us in His Word why He loves us. He asks

us only to believe it. It is both the duty and the privilege of the pastor-counselor to convey this wonderful truth clearly and convincingly to his counselees. Perhaps only God can give the distressed person the sense of "unconditioned acceptance" of which Rogers speaks (see chapter 3, footnote 8).

It is rather significant that such unconditioned acceptance does not always produce the desired changes in the recipients. Just as men regularly disappoint those who truly care about them, so people do not always respond favorably to the love of God.

Divine resources are sufficient to meet man's need
God has the ability to enlighten, to convict of sin, to regenerate and to transform lives. Where willpower fails, God's power succeeds in changing the ingrained habit patterns of many years. A man becomes a new creature in Christ (2 Cor. 5:17).

It is interesting to note that Freud's pessimism about the nature of man and his disregard for God did not logically prevent him from being optimistic about the possibilities of psychoanalysis. Surely the Bible-believing pastor has reason for being optimistic about the effects of Scriptural counseling because of what the grace and power of God can do.

Guilt may be beneficial
While some psychologists believe that guilt feelings are one of the major culprits in mental distress, others see guilt as God's alarm within the mind of man telling him that something needs to be changed.

In his book *Guilt and Grace* Paul Tournier makes a distinction between a false, unnecessary or functional guilt and a true or value guilt. He states:

> A feeling of "functional guilt" is one which results from social suggestion, fear of taboos or of losing the love of others. A feeling of "value guilt" is the genuine consciousness of having betrayed an authentic standard; it is a free judgment of the self by the self . . . "false guilt" comes as a result of the judgments and suggestions of men. "True guilt" is that which results from divine judg-

ment. . . . Therefore real guilt is often something quite different from what constantly weighs us down because of our fear of social judgment and the disapproval of men. We become independent of them in proportion as we depend on God.[22]

In his chapter "The Goodness of Guilt" Drakeford says:

The common notion of guilt is of an unrelenting and tyrannical force, creating misery and unhappiness for man. But this is only part of its role. . . . Without a sense of guilt a Western society deteriorates. . . . In any well ordered society, sociopaths, with their low level of guilt, are so destructive that they have to be placed in a penitentiary or a mental hospital, hopefully to reform them, more realistically, to save the community from their incursions.[23]

In David's account of his transgression concerning Bathsheba and Uriah, it is evident that God used an intensive sense of guilt to bring David to repentance (Ps. 32).

We have seen that the theological presuppositions with which a Biblically-oriented pastor-counselor must work will have a great influence upon his choice of goals, methods and therapeutic approaches for his counseling.

5 Psychological Presuppositions in Pastoral Counseling

The goals, methods, techniques and approaches used in pastoral counseling are all derived from psychological presuppositions. Some writers very clearly spell out their presuppositions; others do not seem to think them important enough to mention. Perhaps some have purposely avoided delineating the beliefs that underlie their psychotherapies.

Since psychological presuppositions have theological implications, a Biblically-oriented pastor will want to discover and understand these presuppositions. He will want to guard against presuppositions of a psychotherapy that are in conflict with Scripture.

There is much difference of opinion among counselors in the area of presuppositions. Therefore, it seems necessary to point out the chief differences between the views of men like Freud, Glasser, Drakeford, Ellis and Adams, who are so strongly influencing the Biblically-oriented pastors of today.

The major psychological presuppositions that I accept are as follows:

The existence of the unconscious

J.P. Chaplin defines the psyche as "the mind, including both conscious and unconscious processes."[1] The psyche is seen as that aspect of the human being that performs psychological functions.

The unconscious is usually defined as that part of the psyche, including memories, perceptions and motivations, that is un-known at least temporarily to the individual. Research on the human brain indicates that the mind can forget nothing perm-anently except in the case of brain damage. Everything that a man's senses have fed into his brain and everything his mind has thought is somehow stored in the cells of the brain. But most of what is stored in our brains is not in our conscious minds. Some of that content is easily brought to consciousness by simple recall, but some of it is buried so deeply that it is very difficult to bring to consciousness.

There is much debate about the nature of the unconscious, so it may be best for our purpose to use the designation "uncon-scious" to refer to any absence of awareness. We can therefore avoid speculating about the nature of unconsciousness without denying its existence.

There are three possible modes for the expression of uncon-scious processes—**mental, somatic** and **social.**

Mental manifestations include such things as forgetting a name, talking in one's sleep, dreaming, slips of the tongue, phob-ias, compulsions and an anxiety for which there seems to be no explanation.

The unconscious shows itself somatically in such physical ailments as ulcers, high blood pressure, diarrhea, colitis, allergies, stomachache, backache, headache and sometimes even cancer.

The social manifestations are the different methods of "acting out"—juvenile delinquency, truancy, crime, drugs, sexual devi-ation and other ways of making life miserable for others.

There is a question as to why certain thoughts are blotted out from awareness. It is believed that some thoughts are too pain-ful or contain too much anxiety or threat to retain them in the conscious mind. The mind's ability to bring about psychological activity to keep unwanted thoughts out of awareness is called **re-pression.** Branden comments upon the extent of one's repression:

> The extent of one's repression and of subsequent psychological
> damage depends upon many factors, such as the magnitude of
> the pain and frustration to which he is subjected, the nature and

extent of any counter-acting benevolent factors in his environment, and very importantly the degree of his will to think, to grow, to develop his power, to transcend his adversity. A child with a strong commitment to remaining in good contact with reality (and there are great differences among children in this regard) will better withstand the impact of a destructive environment than a child whose commitment to reality is more fragile. . . . But some degree of repression in children seems universal.[2]

Whether or not a thought is unconscious has no bearing on its dynamic quality. Some conscious thoughts are not stronger than unconscious ones. Neither is it true that the unconscious thoughts are the real motivators of the mind, while the conscious are relatively unimportant.

Unconscious material that is kept repressed by a strong force usually has only one aim: discharge.[3] It is constantly trying to come to the surface.

Human behavior is determined by motivation, much of which is unconscious

Man's goal-seeking activity is very complex, for he is motivated by many things.

<u>He is motivated by a desire to fulfill various needs.</u> Branden defines a need as "that which an organism requires for its survival or welfare."[4]

Biological needs. Man has a biological need for food, drink, sleep, clothing (in most climates), shelter and oxygen. Much of human behavior can be explained by man's desire to fulfill his biological needs. There is no evidence that sex is a biological need. It may be that sexual behavior is a product of learning—learning so simple for the organism to attain, that virtually all members of the species who develop normally exhibit it. The Bible does not indicate that sexual activity is a biological need. God did not provide a wife for Paul, nor does He make this provision for all people today. He has promised to supply all our needs—and evidently that does not include a mate. Sex is a biological need for the race but not for the individual.

Psychological needs. From the study of the temperaments of identical twins who have been reared separately, it seems evident that genetic inheritance results in differences of psychological need in various individuals.

The need for love and affection is common to each newborn child. What is a need for an infant may be just a very strong desire in an older person. Research indicates clearly that during the first years of a child's life it has a great need to be cared for physically (fed and changed) in a loving way, to be touched, held, talked to and caressed. The mortality rate among unloved children in orphanages is very high. All throughout childhood there is a need to be treated as someone worthwhile, to be listened to and understood, to receive attention and to be treated reasonably and justly. The child needs to feel loved and accepted even when being disciplined. Branden speaks of the long-range devastation that can result from a child's repression of these needs and of the pain associated with their traumatic frustration.[5] The frustration of this need in some has resulted in attention-getting misbehavior. Young ladies who do not receive affection and attention from their fathers sometimes seek affection in a promiscuous sex life. Another result of rejection and disapproval is repressed hostility, a free-floating hostility for which there appears to be no cause.

Many have a sense of inferiority or inadequacy because they did not feel loved. It is this feeling of being "a nobody" that has caused so many to strive relentlessly to become "somebody." Some allow the lack of love to lead them to withdraw from the world around them. They cut themselves off from the love, affection and joy that they really need in their lives.

An individual cannot be psychologically healthy without the positive self-image that results from being treated with love and respect. Man is born with a need to be loved and respected, but he is not born with a knowledge of that need or of how to satisfy it. It is in relation to the satisfying or frustrating of this need that the influence of other persons, especially parents, so powerfully affects our lives. A person's self-image is considered by some to be the most powerful of all motivating factors, for it has a tremendous impact upon his thinking, emotions and behavior.

<u>He is motivated by a pleasure/pain sensory apparatus.</u> A pleasure/pain sensory apparatus produces some behavior that is unlearned, such as man's tendency to move toward warmth. Some examples of learned behavior based upon this sensory apparatus are eating certain foods, drinking certain fluids, indulging in sexual relations and taking a warm bath. This same sensory apparatus causes us to instinctively turn from cold and to avoid such things as a hot stove, thorns and briars or exhausting physical labor.

<u>He is motivated by his values and premises.</u> Values means that which is good or bad or that which is good or bad for me. The emotions and desires that move a man to action are the product of value judgments. All purposeful action aims at the achievement of a value.

Some of these values are innate. Every man has a conscience that either condemns or condones his behavior (Rom. 2:15). Primitive and isolated people who have never heard of the God of the Bible or the law of Moses give evidence of having an inward moral voice. The Chavante Indian tribe with whom I labored in the Amazon Valley of Brazil showed much conviction on their faces as the Ten Commandments were given to them for the first time. Something within them agreed with the outward law of God.

Some of these values are the internalized voice of the parents or of the surrogate parents. The internalizing of parental restrictions is a simple learning process. The child acts on some impulse; the behavior is punished (or punishment is threatened); and this connection with punishment causes the action to be internally inhibited thereafter as a general rule. But it has been observed that the values of some delinquent children showed no internalization of parental attitudes. White assumed that "in such cases the child had not been offered a good bargain: there was too little love to make it worth his while to inhibit things he wanted to do."[6] The internalizing of parental priorities is not automatic either, but they do generally play an important part in the forming of the child's priorities.

Some of these values are of the individual's own choosing. As a child grows and faces various moral situations, he begins to intellectualize and to make choices of his own. When coming under the influence of a new and different culture, society or doctrine, the individual is faced with moral decisions. Often his decisions are not in keeping with his past training.

The individual also makes choices as to what is important in life. Many times things are chosen as values simply because they tend to satisfy needs, either real or imagined.

Instead of seeking to glorify God, many give priority to the meeting of their biological needs and to the psychological need to be loved. These individuals sometimes seek their own satisfaction in material possessions, pleasures, achievements, power or glory.

Because a person can freely make these value judgments, he is in some measure a self-determined being.

Premises. Premises means that which an individual believes to be of factual importance to his behavior. The following premises have a powerful influence upon human behavior:

The existence of God

There is a God before whom we live. Joseph could not commit adultery with Potiphar's wife because he was aware of God.

The fact of resurrection

Man as an individual has been either encouraged or discouraged from a particular course of action because of the belief that he will be raised from the dead some day and will give account of his actions. Some have been encouraged toward faithful service because of a belief in eternal reward (1 Cor. 15:58), and others have been discouraged from serious sin (suicide, adultery, murder) because of a belief in eternal punishment.

The distasteful consequences of sin

When a person is convinced that "the way of the transgressor is hard" it will powerfully influence his life. If he is certain of imprisonment, shame, misery or death he is likely to be greatly inhibited.

<u>Man is sometimes motivated by repressed wishes.</u> It is believed that some of the things that we have forgotten and repressed actually drive us. We are not as fully in control of our motives and actions as we would like to think we are. For example, White tells us that Freud noticed that when his patients were in a positive transference they tended to arrive on time, if not early, for their appointments. During periods of negative transference, they came late and even "forgot" their appointments.[7]

<u>Believers are motivated by the Spirit of God.</u> The Spirit of God using the Word of God motivates us to restrain the desires of the flesh. "This I say then, Walk in the Spirit, and ye shall not fulfil the lust of the flesh" (Gal. 5:16).

The Spirit of God also motivates believers to please and honor Jesus Christ. Our behavior is governed not so much by the "thou shalt nots" as by a desire to please the One Who has done so much for us and Who means so much to us (2 Cor. 5:15).

The Spirit of God gives the power as well as the motivation to do God's pleasure. "For it is God which worketh in you both to will and to do of his good pleasure" (Phil. 2:13).

It is needless to say that some of the above motivations will often be in conflict. The unregenerate man must, as Roberts says, "grope toward a precarious balance between some measure of aggressive self-expression, without which he cannot live at all, and some measure of inhibition, without which he cannot live as a socialized human being."[8] Civilization has been defined as being merely learned restraint. Learned restraint is also a key characteristic of emotional maturity. The Christian who lives according to God's Word and God's Spirit will naturally come to the balanced life, which I believe is the abundant life Jesus Christ promised.

When the human will is subject to the Word of God, conscious motivations will be judged by the Word of God and any sinful unconscious motivations will be held in restraint.

Anxiety is the chief characteristic of psychological disorders

According to Martin Gross, the American Psychiatric Association is planning to eliminate the classification of neuroses from the next edition of its official diagnostic manual and to replace it with the classification "Anxiety Disorders."[9] This change in classification is the result of a growing conviction that anxiety is the key to, or common denominator in, psychological disorders.

Anxiety is defined as "a feeling of mingled dread and apprehension about the future without specific cause for the fear."[10] If a threat is immediate and specific, our emotional reaction is called fear. Anxiety refers to the fear that is provoked not by actual circumstances but by unconscious conflicts. It is often called "floating anxiety" because the person experiencing it cannot tell you its cause, and because it tends to fasten on to any possible situation that gives him an excuse for worrying. The anxiety with which we are primarily concerned is that which is deep enough to produce bodily or behavioral symptoms. It is in a rather desperate attempt to avoid anxiety that crippling symptoms are formed.

Anxiety may come from a variety of sources. Some therapists do not believe that it is important to know from where the anxiety comes. However, I, along with others, believe that in some cases insight can have a very significant part in bringing relief.

The following is an overview of the possible sources of anxiety:

<u>Anxiety may be genetically based.</u> Studies of fraternal and identical twins give a statistical indication of an inherited trait. In studying twins who were in mental distress, it was found that twenty-three percent of the fraternal twins had siblings who shared their condition but with identical twins the rate rose to fifty-two percent.[11]

<u>Anxiety may be related to the birth trauma.</u> Rank taught a mother-centered conception of fear anxiety. He believed that the birth trauma was the most important source of emotional disturbance.[12]

<u>Anxiety may be communicated from a mother.</u> Henry

Laughlin of the Walter Reed Medical Center said:

> The infant possesses a keen ability to sense intuitively the presence
> of all kinds of various emotions including anxiety, indifference,
> resentment, and hatred in the mother or mother figure. . . . The
> presence of anxiety is often communicated from the mother to
> the child automatically and rapidly . . . through his ability to sense
> mood changes, uneasiness, apprehension or anxiety . . . the infant
> has thus another primary pathway for the development of
> anxiety.[13]

<u>Anxiety may develop from a childhood sense of helplessness.</u>
From the time of infancy a child experiences a sense of helplessness and dependency. When he does not get what he wants from
those upon whom he depends, he tends to become anxious and
hostile. And when the hostility is repressed, it too may produce
anxiety.

<u>Anxiety results from man's alienation from God.</u> Man's loss
of faith in God at the time of the Fall resulted in his looking out
for himself. Since man is not able to foresee the future or to control
events, he is anxious about his ability to care for himself.

<u>Anxiety in the unconverted sometimes results from the
threat of nonbeing.</u> Basil Jackson says:

> The mature Christian has, by his faith in Christ, solved the prob-
> lem of existential anguish and despair. His faith has provided him
> with security, and with a general framework for hope within which
> a meaning and purpose for existence can be worked out.[14]

<u>Anxiety may result from a conflict with the culture's mores.</u>
Because of his temperament, a person may be considered very
normal in one culture and yet abnormal in another. In an uncomfortable culture, anxiety is likely to develop.

<u>Anxiety results from irrational thinking.</u> When an individual
perceives something by means of his five senses, he begins to organize and interpret that information. He makes value judgments
about that information. If his value judgments are not in accord
with reality, he is thinking irrationally and anxiety is likely to
result. People are not generally aware of their irrational thinking.

Normal anxiety results from the loss of a loved one or of employment. However, if a person sees himself unrealistically in relation to these situations, an abnormal anxiety will also develop. Included here would be irrational fears that a loved one will be lost through sickness, accident or war.

Anxiety may result from interpersonal relationships. Whether intentional or unintentional, the behavior of other people does not always please us. Sometimes they say and do things that cause us great pain, because we interpret these things as a lack of concern or appreciation for us, or as a downright rejection.

Anxiety may result from physical causes. Pain is well remembered. Fear of its recurrence often brings anxiety.

Anxiety results from fear of losing another's love. Irrational fears about a mate's faithfulness, or a jealous concern about the possible loss of one's popularity to another, results in anxiety.

Anxiety results from the fear of disapproval. "The fear of disapproval by others for what is base and unworthy in one's conduct," says Raymond McCall, "is one of the most powerful motives for human existence, and a plausible basis for that nameless but often unsettling apprehension that we call anxiety."[15]

Anxiety results from feelings of inferiority. When feelings of inferiority are severe and painful, they create unbearable anxiety. The counselee is then driven into overcompensation. He makes excessive and irrational strivings for superiority as a means of defense against anxiety. A child who thinks he is not as strong, intelligent, or attractive as others often overcompensates by competition and aggression.

Milton Layden in his book *Escaping the Hostility Trap* presents a formula that has been very helpful in explaining the consequences of inferiority or low self-esteem.

$$I \Rightarrow A + OB + H + S + MAR$$

I   =the feeling of inferiority or loss of self-respect
$\Rightarrow$ =generates
A   =Anxiety (the fear that one is insufficiently respected)
OB =Obsession with oneself (when one is deprived of self-

respect one becomes obsessed with it)

H   =Hostility

Layden says:

> Hostility is as normal a physiological response as shivering. Just as we shiver in response to sufficient lowering of our temperature, so we become hostile in response to lowering of our self-respect, via any kind of provocation which we interpret as disrespectful. Such provocation may arise from our own thoughts or from the attitudes and feelings of others; they are so frequent that we rarely get through a day without them.[16]

S   =Mirage of Superiority
In order to relieve us of the misery of inferiority, our balancing mechanism provides us with a false sense of superiority, which makes us insist that we are right on most issues.

MAR =Martyring (blaming other persons and situations for our failures)

The anxiety that is derived from inferiority results in several other manifestations:

1. Attention-getting behavior such as complaining of being bored, promiscuity (especially among girls), body-building kicks in boys, beautifying kicks in girls and a constant desire to be in the limelight.

2. Power-seeking behavior such as contrariness, stubbornness, constantly looking for ways to circumvent parental authority (dawdling with the dishes, delaying in the mowing of the lawn), always being late, and a strong drive for political power.

3. Obsessive working—workaholics are seeking to gain approval.

4. Perfectionism—this is an attempt to feel better about oneself.

5. Withdrawing—a shy person or loner does not want to risk rejection.

6. Negative criticism—to the degree that people feel good about themselves, they will not need to put others down.

7. Refusing to attempt a challenging task—failure is so overwhelming that some do not risk beginning a task.

8. Depression—this usually involves anger because someone has attacked our ego, neglected us or failed to show the proper appreciation! A large percentage of depressed people express self-dislike.

9. Alcoholism—often the result of one's dissatisfaction with his status. He often resorts to lies and pretense in order to present the picture of a worthwhile and likable person.

10. Smoking, compulsive gambling and overeating—these often follow the anxiety that is derived from inferiority.

11. Fatigue—inferiority produces anxiety which consumes energy and therefore makes people feel tired.

12. Stupidity—inferiority produces hostility and hostility produces insanity. Sometimes people ask themselves, "How could I have acted so stupidly?" The Watergate affair shows how hostility and resentment brought about a stupid plan.

13. Negative interpretation of future experiences—a low self-image causes a person to interpret in a negative way the various aspects of his interpersonal relationships. It is not what people think of him that counts, but what he thinks they think of him. A low self-image then reinforces itself by causing him to interpret reality in such a way that his self-esteem is lowered still further.

<u>Anxiety results from a conflict of motivations.</u> Man is motivated by needs (both physical and psychological), by his pleasure/pain sensory apparatus, by his values and premises and by the values of his society. In addition to these, the believer is motivated by the Spirit of God (see pages 61–66).

It is obvious that conflicts between these motivations are inevitable at times in every fallible human being. These inevitable conflicts may be considered one of the consequences of original sin. Man is doomed to inner disunity and to the anxiety it brings. Conflict is inevitable when one motivation suggests we do one thing and another motivation suggests we do something else. For example, we can be caught between our needs or desires and our conscience. One says, "I want to" and the other says, "you must not." Cramer uses the story of the old farm horse to illustrate. "Even a tired old farm horse could develop nervous jitters if the driver shouted, 'Gitty-up' and in the same breath tightened the reins and hollered, 'Whoa'."[17]

This is the theory of the "double-bind." Should the individual disregard the "whoa" and actually do what his conscience tells him not to do, guilt and anxiety will result. I agree with Freud that "for any emotional experience to be the source of a psychic disturbance, it had to be strongly distasteful to the individual's conscious self."[18]

It does not seem necessary to limit the cause of anxiety to a solitary factor. There are several causative factors that are common to all men: a sense of helplessness in infancy, alienation from God, the threat of nonbeing, irrational thinking and a conflict of motivations. It is quite likely that most persons will also suffer from unsatisfactory interpersonal relationships, fear of disapproval and feelings of inferiority.

The result of limiting oneself to just one cause of anxiety is that the counselor might fail often in his diagnoses. Without a proper diagnosis, how can he know how to bring the resources of God to bear upon the problem?

Man develops defense mechanisms in order to deal with anxiety and to lower tensions

Anxiety is a danger signal that something is wrong either externally or internally. Open awareness of the anxiety and its cause may help one to find a solution to the problem that induced the anxiety. Realistically acknowledging a deficiency and attempting on a conscious level to modify the defect is called **coping**.

When an individual does not want to honestly face up to his defect because he fears it will bring a painful loss of self-esteem, the ego unconsciously chooses a mechanism of defense. The ego's application of these defense mechanisms is a rather desperate attempt to avoid or defend against feelings of guilt or shame. Usually more than one defense mechanism is found operating at the same time; rarely are they found singly.

Since the essence of psychopathology (emotional illness) is dishonesty, it is imperative that a counselor has a knowledge of the defense mechanisms so that he might be able to bring the person to an honest and realistic appraisal of both himself and his situation. We shall consider the following defense mechanisms:

<u>Denial.</u> When facing an external threat, stress or danger, some people (usually children or those with weak egos) react simply by denying the existing threat. Only those who can tolerate the side-by-side existence of a pretend world and a real world are able to make use of the mechanism of denial. White says:

> If the person cannot escape or attack the threat, the only bearable alternative is to deny it. Thus a baby carried into a room full of strangers may simply gaze at the door until he musters courage to peek at some of the unknown faces.[19]

<u>Repression.</u> When facing something within ourselves that poses a threat, repression is the first defense mechanism called into play. It is basically a denial or ejection from awareness of such thoughts as shameful memories and unacceptable motives. The other defense mechanisms aimed at internal threats are used only when repression proves to be inadequate. All other defense mechanisms are dependent on some initial repression. Only when an unacceptable thought is removed from consciousness can other mechanisms be utilized against it. Jackson, illustrating repression, says:

> Suppose, for example, that the object of my hostility is not just anyone, but my father. This desire would go so much against what I believe to be right and appropriate that I refuse to even permit the thought into consciousness. At the first evidence of it, I immediately, automatically and unconsciously force it out of my conscious awareness. This is repression.[20]

<u>Isolation.</u> Isolation essentially is keeping apart that which belongs together. For example, "to avoid guilt, the person splits his motive away from objectionable actions. A man plunges a knife into someone without thinking of the act."[21] Another

example is the splitting of emotion from thought. A woman hears devastating news and breaks into hysterical laughter. A physician working in the emergency room of a hospital needs the mechanism of isolation in order to function properly.

<u>Reaction formation.</u> Reaction formation is an effort to maintain repression of a forbidden wish or impulse by unconsciously seeking to cultivate personality traits, attitudes and habits that are the opposite or antithesis of the forbidden impulse. A mother unconsciously rejects her child. Since she cannot accept her conscious feelings she overprotects the child, thereby attempting to prove by the opposite feeling that the original one does not exist. Another person has a strong desire to kill or hurt, so he becomes a pacifist.

<u>Rationalization.</u> Rationalization is a clearly conscious attempt to explain away or justify something unacceptable—an undesirable action is ascribed to an acceptable motive. It involves telling yourself an unconscious lie or kidding yourself. A man doesn't want to become a minister because of the prospect of low pay and high pressure, so he tells himself and others that he can do more for the cause of Christ by being a prosperous businessman.

<u>Undoing.</u> Undoing is an attempt by some means of symbolic restitution to make atonement for a present forbidden impulse or a past unacceptable behavior. This defense is a common basis for the obsessive-compulsive symptom complex. It is a very common idea that suffering, in some magical way, atones for or nullifies evil. This idea is the psychological basis for the religious practice of flagellation.

<u>Identification.</u> When a person defends against anxiety that is associated with personal inadequacy, he may view or mold himself in the likeness of someone he perceives as having adequacy, power and status. By means of identification a child acquires the characteristics of a parent or a teacher. Identification is also important to the development of the conscience. There are three special types of identification:

1. *Incorporation.* In incorporation, the whole psychic image of the one he perceives to be adequate becomes part of the individual's personality. An Indian in the jungles of South America feels inadequate, making him anxious. He sees a jaguar, which to him is the epitome of courage and strength; so he kills it and eats its heart, thinking it to be the repository of the jaguar's courage.

2. *Introjection.* This is the symbolic assimilation of the loved or hated external object. As part of our development we introject, or incorporate into our personalities, the standards and values of our parents. I do not do certain things not because daddy said so, but because I, myself, do not want to do them since I am like my father.

3. *Identification with the aggressor.* To defend against the anxiety of being aggressed against, the ego uses the mechanism of identification with the aggressor. If we become like the aggressor—having his strength, status and power—then we will have no reason to be afraid. Some Jews in the Nazi death camps identified with their enemies and persecuted their fellow prisoners. Some of the most vicious prejudice against blacks has been manifested by lighter-skinned blacks.

<u>Displacement.</u> Displacement is the shifting of an unacceptable motive and its associated effect to a substitute object that may provide some release.

Sometimes the displacement is symbolic. A man is angry with his friend because his friend's adequacy is a threat to his own self-esteem, so he plans and practices hard to beat him at tennis. The unusual pleasure from beating the friend at the game is a clue that displacement is taking place. Symbolic displacement also occurs when a man is angry with his boss but feels too threatened to let him know it; so when he gets home he is very irritable with his family.

<u>Symbolization.</u> Symbolization is the mechanism by which one idea or object is used to represent another idea or object. It defends against anxiety because we can tolerate the chosen symbol without experiencing significant degrees of anxiety. Sym-

bolization is the common language of the unconscious, as in our dreams.

> This mechanism is being utilized in phobias. When a person shows great fear of something that is, in fact, perfectly harmless, we have to assume that the real threat lies somewhere else. The phobic object is serving as a symbol or a distant reminder of some danger that is extremely real to the patient, even though its origin may have been in childhood.[22]

<u>Defensive discounting.</u> Defensive discounting occurs when a person defends against his own defects and inadequacies and seeks to relieve his anxiety by focusing on the inadequacies of others.

The person who is a constant complainer and faultfinder is likely to have a lack of insight into his own personal inadequacies.

<u>Regression.</u> Regression is a return to an earlier emotional and developmental level where there is much less to provoke anxiety and it is easier to find gratification. The alcoholic regresses to an oral method of dealing with anxiety. In severe cases of schizophrenia there is a return to a state of near primary narcissism. A physically ill person often wants to be nursed and babied to some degree.

<u>Intellectualization.</u> This is the overaccentuation and use of intellectual concepts and vocabulary to defend oneself against the anxiety of a particular experience or situation. "There is a tendency to take emotional conflicts into the sphere of the intellect, divest them of affective and personal meaning, and work on them as problems in metaphysics, religion, or political theory."[23]

An adolescent may become absorbed in the pursuit of existential philosophy to "take his mind off" the anxiety associated with sexual feelings.

<u>Compensation.</u> In compensation one goal or motive is overaccentuated as a means of defending against the anxiety that results from an acknowledged deficiency. A young man has an intellectual weakness that causes him distress, so he works hard at becoming a super athlete.

Projection. Projection is used to attribute our own unacceptable thoughts and feelings to others. It is basic to paranoid conditions and to delusions and hallucinations. Projection is characterized by absence of insight and is the core of much malignant psychopathology.

Often our critical appraisal of someone else is a cover-up and is actually a recital of our own mistakes in disguise.[24]

Autistic fantasy and substitution. Autistic fantasy is a special kind of withdrawal in which a fantasy is substituted for fact to defend against the anxiety of low self-esteem, inadequacy and failure. Autistic fantasy and substitution differs from ordinary daydreaming in that it acts to avoid action rather than to prepare for it. A child who does not receive much attention may daydream about being a military hero returning from war, riding in a victory parade and receiving much honor.

Sublimation. Sublimation, a very important defense mechanism, is a means whereby consciously unacceptable impulses are redirected into acceptable channels. A child who loved knives and possessed a great deal of aggression and hostility became a highly successful and respected surgeon.

Sublimation is the process whereby fierce and aggressive dogs become tamed, but energetic, sled dogs.

Endo-psychic withdrawal. In endo-psychic withdrawal the individual removes himself psychologically, not physically, from a goal that is considered to be deserved but not attainable. He does so by unconsciously giving up any interest in, or desire for, the unattainable goal.

In coping we consciously limit ourselves to what is realistically obtainable, whereas in withdrawal we use dishonesty by saying that we do not desire the goal that is unattainable.

Jackson gives this example:

I want to be President of the United States. I have an awareness that I don't have the ability. This threatens my self-esteem. Anxiety is produced—so I endo-psychically withdraw and convince myself that no one in his right mind would be interested in being President since all politicians are crooked.[25]

Symptoms are the surface phenomena of psychological disorders

The phenomenology of a psychological disorder is the totality of its external manifestations. It is a psychological fact that unconscious psychological needs tend to push their way up into consciousness and to manifest themselves externally. These external manifestations are called symptoms and are based on insufficiencies of the normal control apparatus. These insufficiencies can be brought on by too much excitation (traumatic experiences) or by a previous damming up of tensions that causes normal excitations to act like traumatic ones.[26]

Symptoms of psychological disorders tell us nothing about causes. They make very little sense when they are studied apart from their determinants. They are a reflection of either the anxiety reaction itself, or the defense mechanism, or the impulses in the patient that create anxiety.[27] The nucleus of anxiety, defense mechanisms, conflict, protective organization and psychological breakdown must all be understood before it is possible to make sense of symptom formations.

Symptoms of psychological disorders fall into three natural groupings: mental, somatic and social.

Mental symptoms. There are several mental symptoms of psychological disorder. However, there is a problem in classifying some of them so as to make clear-cut distinctions between them. Fortunately, psychological disorders can be well understood and effectively treated even when the symptom picture is confusing.

The following are the various categories of mental symptoms as set forth by Jackson.[28]

Simple anxiety disorders. These disorders refer to anxiety attacks in which one's fears grow altogether beyond his control. Usually the person does not know precisely of what he is afraid, but his body reacts just as it would to an outward physical threat. Since there is no definite external threat to face, the person cannot act. Therefore, he remains in a constant state of vigilance, which has its physical symptoms: palpitations, headaches, dizziness, digestive upsets, breathlessness, an unassuageable thirst and various pains caused by muscular tension.

The chronic anxiety, out of which the acute attack ordinarily arises, also has somatic manifestations—tremor of hands or lips, table drumming, foot tapping, clenching of the teeth, tugging and smoothing of clothing and hair, fidgeting, pacing, facial tics and grimaces, licking of lips and the clearing of the throat.[29]

Phobic disorder. A phobia is an intense fear of an object or situation intellectually recognized as not truly dangerous. It is the result of displacement, that is, one's unconscious fear of an original object or situation is attached symbolically to a new object, one that is within the individual's power to avoid. The fear is kept under some degree of control without having to face up to it realistically.[30]

Some of the most common phobias are: acrophobia (fear of heights), claustrophobia (being in a close space), agoraphobia (going out on the street alone), mysophobia (fear of dirt or germs), hematophobia (fear of blood), pyrophobia (fear of fire), ophidiophobia (fear of snakes) and ailurophobia (fear of cats).

Depressive disorder. White describes "depressive" as "feeling deserted and despairing, sinful and worthless, unlovable and deserving of the utmost punishment."[31] This disorder seems to be based on an exaggerated response to the loss of a loved one, or misfortune. The exaggeration is determined by personal history, which has given situations of this kind a heavy loading of threat. The patient is peculiarly sensitive to desertion or loss, either because of happenings over which he has no control or because of the consequences of his own hostility. When real situations of this kind occur, or when his human relationships take a turn that he can interpret as loss or desertion, he begins to manifest the symptoms of depression.

Obsessive-compulsive disorder. "An obsession is an idea or desire which forces itself persistently into the patient's mind in what he experiences as an irrational fashion."[32] Obsessions intrude themselves without any known reason. If a person tries to discontinue his obsessive thinking, he suffers an attack of anxiety.

Some obsessions give expression to aggressive impulses such

as murderous hostility. Some express sexual urges in a crude and violent form, and others give expression to self-corrective tendencies such as orderliness, cleanliness, propitiatory acts or self-imposed duties.

In cases of obsessions, the underlying problem is represented in consciousness more fully than are other cases of psychological disorder.

A compulsion is a sequence of actions one feels compelled to carry out precisely even though one recognizes their irrational nature. McCall tells of a woman who felt compelled to bathe and dress herself according to a very exact procedure. On one occasion she undressed and bathed herself five times in succession, while her husband waited to take her out for dinner.[33]

Another common example of compulsion is that of hand-washing, which often is related to sexual transgressions during one's youth. The compulsion to arrange such things as clothes, books, papers and pictures in an exact order is also common.

Hysterical disorder. Hysteria refers to such symptoms as conversion and dissociation and is found in highly immature, highly suggestible, self-centered and self-dramatizing personalities.

In conversion, there is such a close link between the psychic and the somatic that hysteria can readily convert a psychological problem into an apparent physical disability. This would include such manifestations as blindness, loss of voice and paralysis. People who exhibit conversion seem to be free from anxiety and hostility and appear to be unconcerned about their physical problem. Putting up with a physical problem relieves them of facing the underlying psychic problem. The hysteric has a great capacity for self-deception and a tendency to obscure the dividing line between fantasy and reality.

In the dissociate type of hysteria, the individual blocks off from awareness a significant portion of his present experience.[34] When the blocked-off portion is in control, he is in a state of dissociation.

Some examples of dissociation are sleep-walking, amnesia and multiple-personality.

<u>Somatic Symptoms.</u> The following are possible physical manifestations of psychological disorders: obesity, sustained loss of appetite, peptic ulcer, ulcerative colitis, high blood pressure, unconsciousness, migraine headache, hyperventilation, bronchial asthma, menstrual disorders, menopausal disorders, frigidity, impotence, functional backache, tension headache, rheumatoid arthritis, certain skin reactions, loss of sight, loss of voice, loss of the use of a limb and even cancer.

Research has found that cancer patients tend to be highly repressed and to deny stress, which lends support to the idea that repressed persons may be cancer-prone. It has been observed by cancer researcher Vernon Riley, in his tests on mice, that:

> As a response to anxiety there is a marked increase in the secretion of corticosterone from the adrenal cortex under activation by the hypothalmus of the brain. This increase in corticosterone levels results in a dramatic lowering of the body's immune response to disease as a result of a reduction in the number of circulating lymphocytes (white blood cells that fight invading germs), a decrease in the size of the thymus, a gland that is intimately involved in disease resistance, and a loss in the tissue mass of the spleen and lymph nodes.[35]

We can easily see, then, the truth of Proverbs 17:22, "A merry heart doeth good like a medicine. . . ."

<u>Social symptoms.</u> Instead of suffering personally with either mental or somatic disorders, some disturbed individuals make other people suffer by acting out or carrying into action their repressed impulses. These are people who are abnormal in terms of society—not conforming to the prevailing cultural milieu.[36] This category includes criminals, delinquents, alcoholics, drug addicts and sexual deviates.

Insight is often useful in bringing about relief from mental distress

This is one of the most disputed of psychological assumptions. It is directly related to the question of the value of dealing with a person's past. Clinebell quotes W. Menninger as saying,

"It isn't necessary to know how a fire started in order to put it out."[37] Glasser, who strongly argues against the value of case histories, says:

> The most complete history possible, perhaps a sound motion picture of the patient's whole life plus a tape-recording of every unconscious thought, would be no more helpful in treating a patient, than a short description of his present problem.[38]

However, even those who major on the present admit to some value in going into a counselee's life history. After strongly disparaging the need for going into one's past, Glasser states:

> As therapists, however, we do find it helpful to find out how long his current problem has been going on, not for historical information but to help us gauge whether he will need brief or more extended therapy. For example, if a young patient is failing in school, we might want to know how long he has been failing. If it has been going on for a long time, attaining involvement will be more difficult, and therapy will be more intense and take longer than if it is a recent occurrence.[39]

Adams believes that it is important to learn the past well enough to establish that sinful responses are at the root of the present problems.[40] He gives other reasons for obtaining a behavioral history: to determine the life-style of the client, and to help the counselee discover any sins of the past which continue to affect the present.[41]

Hyder, who agrees with Glasser generally, places a stronger emphasis upon the past, believing that it is necessary to take an extensive initial history in the early sessions. Hyder says:

> First, the doctor has to acquire a thorough understanding of the patient as a person, his personality structure, what his family background and upbringing was like, what his present life circumstances are at home, work, and in society, what his present problems are and how they developed, and why he came to get help at this time.[42]

A counselor who has a real concern for a person will want

to know the individual's personal history as well as his present problems.

One of Glasser's main arguments against digging deeply into the past is that some counselees find excuses in the past for their present irresponsible behavior. It could be replied that such people are likely to make excuses for themselves anyway, and that a realistic and responsible view of the past may be just what the counselee needs.

The greatest difference of opinion pertains to the unconscious past of the counselee. Freudian or conventional psychiatry teaches that when a patient gains insight into his past, changes in behavior will automatically come. However, very seldom does this seem to be the case.

There are many psychiatrists who believe strongly in the value of insight who do not think that insight itself brings a cure. Jackson believes that insight into the roots of a problem simply prepares the way to rationally do something about the problem.[43] In other words, insight is not the cure as some formerly thought; it is simply putting the problem in focus. Unless insight is translated into appropriate action, it will be of no value in helping a person successfully handle future stresses.

The essence of insight is making the unconscious to become conscious. It is a sudden glimpse of the obvious; it is seeing what has long been obvious to the counselor or even to others.[44] Insight involves the counselee seeing himself as he really is, discovering the irrational, or possibly satanically inspired, ideas underlying his emotional disturbance. It also involves discovering the unconscious means used by the ego to defend against anxiety; discerning the reason why a particular defense mechanism was chosen; learning how past experience influences present behavior and facing up to his self-deception or dishonesty.

Insight usually takes place within an interpersonal encounter between counselee and counselor or between man and God. It arises out of a sense of dissatisfaction with the present condition and results in a renewal of hope. It is often accompanied by a degree of "reliving past traumas" or "emotional catharsis."[45]

The prodigal son may be said to have experienced insight when he "came to himself" (Luke 15:17). He realized his desperate need, how his friends had deserted him, what his father could do for him and how sinfully he had acted toward his father and toward God. Notice that the prodigal's insight was firsthand, not something imposed upon him by others. Firsthand insight is involved in every Scriptural conversion.

The value of firsthand insight is explained by Roberts:

> When someone else attempts to tell him what his deficiencies are, it makes no difference whether the individual agrees with the other's judgment or not; he is deprived of the opportunity for firsthand insight which is an indispensable part of the healing process. Furthermore, this facing of shortcomings is never constructive unless it can be carried through in a situation where a man is accepted in spite of them, and where the remedy, insofar as one is forthcoming, consists of a dynamic realignment within the person himself instead of something imposed upon him from outside.[46]

We can easily see the implications here concerning high-pressure evangelism. When someone is trying to make us see something, a struggle of wills results; but when a person willingly makes an insight of his own, it has great healing value.[47]

It is interesting to note that once the new emphasis upon insight was considered an improvement upon the old advice-giving or problem-solving approach.[48] Now the trend seems to be away from insight and back to verbal confrontation and advice giving.

Those who argue against the insight approach usually make much of the time element involved. All would agree that classical psychoanalysis is a lengthy procedure; but many believe that a great expenditure of time is not necessary to recover the unconscious material that is vital to insight. Ellis, in answering the question, How can we learn to control and change the thoughts that create our feelings, if we have these thoughts buried deeply in our unconscious minds? states the following:

> What the orthodox Freudians and many other psychoanalysts

keep referring to as "deeply unconscious thoughts" emerge, in the vast majority of cases, as what Freud originally called preconscious ideas. We don't have these thoughts and feelings *immediately* accessible to our awareness. But we can fairly easily learn to infer and observe them, by working back from the behavior which they induce.[49]

As we mentioned before, those who argue against the value of insight claim it gives the counselee more excuses for his irresponsible behavior. This argument would be valid if we accepted the Freudian position of blaming a person's present problems on his parents or other significant persons of his childhood. Part of insight is recognizing one's own responsibility for thinking irrational thoughts and making irresponsible choices.

Glasser says, in effect, forget the past, do not worry about insight, just encourage people to act responsibly in order to fulfill their present needs. Those who are convinced of the value of insight would ask, How can one act to fulfill needs of which he may not be aware? It is as one becomes aware of his real, basic needs that they are met with less effort, and there is less drive to satisfy symbolic desires. The problem of a lack of awareness is set forth by Branden:

> But whereas a person engaged in problem solving is generally able to describe the thoughts and issues with which he is occupied, and a person engaged in action is able to know and state the nature of the action he is performing, most people do not enjoy any comparable facility in describing the nature and content of their emotional experience. And more: There are many instances in which they clearly have a block against doing so. They are not *real* to themselves, which is to say: There is a solid wall standing between their conscious awareness and their immediate internal psychological states.[50]

If Branden is correct about the solid wall standing between one's conscious awareness and his immediate internal psychological state, then Glasser's emphasis upon conscious needs would not seem to be an entirely thorough or sufficient approach.

How can one act responsibly if he is unaware of the actions

by which he keeps his problems alive and flourishing, or if he is unaware of the motivations of his actions?[51]

In speaking of self-esteem Branden says:

> One of the tragedies of human development is that many of a person's most self-destructive acts are prompted by a blind, misguided (and sub-conscious) attempt to protect his sense of self— to preserve or strengthen his self-esteem.[52]

In speaking of "the most effective therapy," Branden states that it involves

> A fairly constant shift of concern, back and forth, between the past and the present—on the one hand guiding the client to re-experience and recognize the meaning of traumatic childhood events, and on the other hand guiding him to an awarenesss of the neurotic blocks and defenses that cripple him as an adult— thereby assisting him to achieve better integration of his life experiences.[53]

After considering the arguments concerning insight, it appears that the counselor should obtain a fairly complete case history and use whatever uncovering techniques he needs to produce insight in the counselee and to give him enough information to evaluate and counsel as he ought.

The pastor-counselor, because of other demands upon his time, should avoid the lengthy process of digging deeply into the counselee's obscure past.

A major source of emotional distress results from attempts to defend our self-esteem

The principle of self-preservation is just as operative on the psychological level as it is on the physical level. Man feels a great need to think well of himself and to protect himself against anything that threatens his self-esteem.

Man's almost unconscious need to preserve his self-esteem seems to be justified by the profound influence it has upon every aspect of his life: his emotions, his desires, his ambitions, his physical health, his choice of values, his productive activity, his sexual romantic responses, his ability to relate to others and even his religious experiences. Branden says, "Self-esteem is the single most eloquent key to man's behavior."[54]

The results of a poor self-concept are listed by Harper: timidity, feelings of inadequacy, outward directed hostility, and inward directed hostility which manifests itself in morbid fears, paranoid tendencies, and depression states.[55]

We fear rejection, anger, censure and criticism, but we crave love and acceptance. Because of this we want to be well-thought of; we are concerned about what others think of us. And because we need so much to have others think well of us, we hesitate to let others know what we are really like deep down inside. We think that it would be disastrous for people to know our true feelings and motives, for then they would judge us as being "bad" or unworthy. We have come to think that we cannot afford to be our real selves.

All our lives we are trying to live up to certain roles and expectations. William Fitts gives a very clear explanation of how our role playing results in a kind of alienation or estrangement from ourselves. He writes:

> We are forever playing roles. Some of us are so fearful lest we not succeed in these roles that we develop innumerable devices for deceiving others—devices for not letting others see our weaknesses and inadequacies.
>
> The tragedy is that in the long run we succeed even more in deceiving ourselves than deceiving others, and we end up as strangers to ourselves. We do not know who we are or what we are really like. Major parts of ourselves have been hidden from others for so long that they are now hidden from us, too. Feelings and emotions, impulses and motives have been driven underground and kept bottled up, and they are no longer a freely functioning part of us. This is not to say that they are no longer with us. In fact they are very much with us. The trouble is that we have no direct access to them and therefore cannot control them. Instead they tend to control us. We find ourselves thinking, saying, feeling, or doing things which we don't mean and can't quite understand. . . . Or possibly these hidden areas of ourselves exert

their forces through physical channels, and we have unaccountable headaches, backaches, stomach pains, or dizzy spells. We have estranged ourselves and defeated ourselves in our efforts to deceive others.[56]

In light of the profound influence of self-esteem on every area and aspect of one's life, it is imperative that a counselor seek to develop in his counselees a sane and Scriptural self-image. The counselor must convey to the counselee in as many ways as are possible and appropriate the fact that he is a significant and worthwhile human being. The Scriptural view of everyone is that he is highly significant, deeply fallen and greatly loved. Those troubled with a low self-image need to be reminded that:

1. Man was made originally in the image of God and "very good" (Gen. 1:26, 31).

2. Man was made a little lower than the angels (Ps. 8:4, 5).

3. Individuals are formed by God (Ps. 139:14).

4. God has eternally identified Himself with man (not angels) by means of the incarnation.

5. God paid a tremendous price to redeem us.

6. Sinful men can become the children of God.

7. Believers become heirs of God and joint-heirs with Christ (Rom. 8:17).

8. Believers are servants of God (Rom. 6:22).

9. Believers are ambassadors for Christ (2 Cor. 5:20).

10. Believers have angelic guardians (Ps. 91:11).

11. God will spend eternity with the redeemed (Rev. 21:3).

Reason is man's basic tool to regain mental peace Assuming that mental peace and wholeness depend upon an integration of all that a man is mentally, emotionally, physically, spiritually and socially, it is very important that we discover the means for bringing about this integration. Canon's law states that the aim of behavior is to maintain tension at its lowest point.[57] The greater the integration of one's personality, the less the tension.

<u>Other opinions.</u> Psychologists differ greatly as to what is the primary means of integration. Consider the following opinions:

Start acting on the basis of feeling. Some believe that the healthy person is one who acts on spontaneous feeling; he acts without thinking. But it is doubtful that there would be such a thing as civilization if people were not thinking before acting— nor could there be any Biblical morality. In fact, an individual could not survive without the kind of thinking that restrains action. Outler claims that, "the organism cannot survive unless its heedless desires are curbed and patterns of constraint and direction are set up."[58]

Start acting responsibly to fulfill your needs.[59] This approach of Glasser's can be effective only if reason, based upon Scripture, is used to discern just what responsible behavior is and to learn what are the needs of which the counselee is entirely unaware. Actually, what is responsible and need-fulfilling may be entirely contrary to what he is feeling, and it may be very difficult to persuade him to act responsibly unless his reason has been convinced that such action is both responsible and rewarding.

This is in fact what Glasser aims for. He says:

> Once we are involved with the patient, we begin to point out to him the unrealistic aspects of his irresponsible behavior. If the patient wishes to argue that his conception of reality is correct, we must be willing to discuss his opinions, but we must not fail to emphasize that our main interest is his behavior rather than his attitude. . . . The patient rather than the therapist must decide whether his behavior is irresponsible or not and whether he should change it. If a boy thinks that he cannot help stealing cars, no therapy is possible. If a man thinks that it is all right to overeat and be fat, no obesity treatment will work. The skill of therapy is to put the responsibility upon the patient . . . The proper function of any treatment institution is to provide a warm, disciplined atmosphere in which the inmates are required to assess their behavior in terms of responsibility.[60]

It seems evident that Glasser places greater emphasis upon changing thinking and attitudes than he admits. But his strong emphasis upon reality, right and wrong and responsibility indicates that his approach is based upon the view that the so-called symptoms (irresponsible behavior) are the illness.[61]

This position is Scripturally untenable, for the Bible places a greater importance upon what a man is inside than upon his outward behavior. The following verses substantiate this view:

> Keep thy heart with all diligence; for out of it are the issues of life (Prov. 4:23).

> For as he thinketh in his heart, so is he (Prov. 23:7).

> O generation of vipers, how can ye, being evil, speak good things? for out of the abundance of the heart the mouth speaketh. A good man out of the good treasure of the heart bringeth forth good things: and an evil man out of the evil treasure bringeth forth evil things (Matt. 12:34, 35).

> For out of the heart proceed evil thoughts, murders, adulteries, fornications, thefts, false witness, blasphemies (Matt. 15:19).

> Woe unto you, scribes and Pharisees, hypocrites! for ye are like unto whited sepulchres, which indeed appear beautiful outward, but are within full of dead men's bones, and of all uncleanness (Matt. 23:27).

The following are Biblical words that indicate heart attitudes that result in irresponsible or sinful behavior: pride, selfishness, lust, stubbornness, anger, dishonesty, bitterness and anxiety.

Clinebell's position follows closely that of Glasser. He holds that the master goal of counseling is to enhance a person's ability to relate to others in more need-satisfying ways and fewer need-depriving ways.[62] And, too, he places a great emphasis upon teaching, which indicates a cognitive approach. The following paragraph, although written by Clinebell, could very well have been written by Ellis.

> The pastor who uses the revised model is more apt to confront the person (within a strong counseling relationship) with the need to face his unconstructive patterns of living. Living in self-contradictory ways which violate one's sense of justice, integrity, and respect for persons is seen as a *cause* and not just a *symptom*

of inner conflict. Many people are capable of making constructive changes in this behavior, whether or not their inner conflicts are resolved. Therefore, the person's guiding values and the behavior resulting therefrom should be examined, not just in terms of how he *feels* about these matters, (although this is important), but also in terms of how they influence his relationships and sense of worth, and what he can *do* to live more constructively.[63]

Express your feelings freely. Pearl's Gestalt theory emphasizes feelings and opposes thinking. Our reason is blamed for our painful human condition. James Sire summarizes this anti-intellectual position:

> Personal experience and feeling are placed above reason, because reason led man to conclude he was not worth anything; new consciousness questions the validity of reason. One jumps from reason to something that will give value. It is usually a kind of mystical leap. One is valuable because he feels himself to be valuable.[64]

Some psychologists see emotional disorder as basically a disordering of feelings. Emotional disordering is caused when a person cannot express or fully experience his feelings. When a person lives from his *present* feelings (sensations with meanings), he is emotionally ordered. If he lives from feelings that *come from the past* (feelings resulting from conscience, parental influence, religious influences) he is emotionally disordered. Since most overpowering feelings of the past come from one's childhood, it is necessary to relive childhood traumas (abreaction) to become free of their influence. The counselee must not only remember and report experiences in which his feelings were blocked but actually express the sadness, anger, hurt or other emotions that were originally present.[65]

It is claimed that abreaction gives tension release and insight into those fixed patterns of behavior that originated in the client's past. He is taught to counteract any feeling expressions or defense that comes from the past. He is taught to proact—express present feelings with present meanings. Hart claims that "together abreaction—counteraction—proaction, constitute a dynamic that allows the patient to progressively integrate his life."[66] To gain and retain this integration, an open-ended therapeutic community is required.

Bruce Maliver strongly disputes the idea that expression of emotion is in itself curative. He says, "The fact is that emotional expression alone . . . was long ago shown to have no lasting effect on the personality."[67]

It remains a question as to whether people who have undergone this therapy can continue to live by its teachings after they have left their therapeutic community.

Since feelings are sensations with meanings, and clients are taught to counteract any feeling expressions that come from the past, is this not a form of brainwashing—substituting the therapist's meanings for those of the parents?

Ellis does not oppose abreaction but believes that expressing and revealing one's feelings may be an important part of therapy "if it is accompanied by a more mature outlook that helps you change some of those very feelings you acknowledge and express."[68]

The Christian should have no opposition to abreaction as long as it does not involve (as it often does in secular therapy) an expression of what the Bible would call sinful attitudes.

It is not denied that sometimes our feelings tend to influence our perception of the world. An example of this is the mechanism of projection which is the attributing of our own thoughts and feelings to other people. The question remains: Can we change emotions without dealing with the thinking or beliefs that are behind them?

Freud's psychoanalysis is based upon the assumption that painful emotions are eliminated by reexperiencing them. The patient relives the experiences that were so painful they were repressed. In so doing, it is hoped that the counselee can "learn to sort out the distortions and inappropriate reactions and find better ways of feeling and living."[69] It appears that Freud's aim is the same as Ellis's: to discover the irrationality of one's earlier emotional responses. Both seek insight but by different methods. Freud believed that insight itself would bring cure, but Ellis believed that insight only prepared the way to making rational choices in the present.

Importance of reason. Reason or thinking changes emotion. A good and easily understood definition of emotion is given by Branden: "An emotion is the psychosomatic form in which a person experiences *his estimate* of the beneficial or harmful relationship of some aspect of reality to himself."[70] An emotion, then, is an implicit value-response—something is either "for me or against me."

One of the therapist's first responsibilities is to teach counselees that their emotions have intelligible causes. We feel the way we do because we think the way we do. Outside circumstances do not magically make us feel the way we do. We disturb ourselves by the way we interpret what we perceive. Man can alter his desires and emotions only by revising the thinking or nonthinking that produced his values and premises. Since much thinking is learned behavior, it can also be unlearned.

Branden believes that a species' distinctive means of survival, of coping with its environment, gives us a clue as to its motivations. And since reason is man's distinctive means of survival, it must have an important part to play in human behavior.[71]

Reason is vital in bringing about emotional peace because:

1. Reason enables man to establish the values by which he evaluates experiences as being either for or against him.

2. Reason enables man to translate needs into goals.

3. Reason enables man to discover repressed desires. (Glasser's emphasis upon behavior fails here.)

4. Reason enables man to alleviate pain and to achieve pleasure.

5. Reason enables man to maintain a cognitive contact with reality.

The reason or value judgment that is part of an emotion is in the form of self-talk. The sentences we are telling ourselves determine our behavior.

It is true then that "the thought is the father to the deed." But it is in regard to *reason* that the cognitive therapist must heed a much-needed warning: He is not to put too much confidence in *unaided reason.* Unlike Thomas Aquinas, who had an undue confidence in Aristotelian logic, most conservative Christian theologians would hold to the view that man's reason has been affected by the fall of Adam; therefore, man's thinking is often contrary to God's thinking (Rom. 8:7) and is often perverted and distorted (Rom. 1:28). It is pure humanism to say, as do some cognitive therapists, that we ourselves are makers of ourselves by means of the thoughts that we choose and encourage and to which we expose ourselves. It is of vital importance that we recognize our responsibility for our ways of thinking. However, it is also very important that we recognize that the unregenerate man's thinking is *not* entirely free—man's reason, too, has been brought into bondage. Therefore, the person whose mind is set free by the regenerating power of the Holy Spirit is the one who will benefit most from cognitive therapy.

When our self-talk is rational and Scriptural (in accordance with both natural and Spiritual realities), then our emotions will be healed and our behavior will become responsible. If the believer's reason is not aided and guided by the Scriptures and the Spirit of God, his trust is really in himself, not in God. Satan would have us put our trust in ourselves so he can keep us in defeat.

Openness

Openness with significant others is the individual's first step on the road back to normality.[72] It is vital to restoring emotional order because it was secrecy and dishonesty that brought on the disorder. Drakeford quotes Jung as saying:

> As soon as man was capable of conceiving the idea of sin, he had recourse to psychic concealment—or, to put it in analytical language, repressions arose. Anything that is concealed is a secret. The maintenance of secrets acts like a psychic poison which alienates their possessor from the community.[73]

The value of openness or confession is set forth in Scripture (Ps. 32:5; 51:1–3; 1 John 1:9). The fifth step of Alcoholics Anonymous is "Admitted to God, to ourselves, and to another human being the exact nature of our wrongs."

Many of the psychotherapies, according to Harper, make use of the therapeutic tool of confession:

> Another component frequently found in psychotherapeutic process is what is generally called *catharsis*. The release of pent-up feelings, the revelation of emotional secrets, in the warm and understanding presence of the therapist are generally helpful to the patient. Disappointment, anxiety, and frustration soon reach intolerable levels in many disturbed persons, and the verbal expression of these feelings sometimes helps to dispel them.[74]

Not only are secrecy and dishonesty causes of emotional disorder, they are also factors in covering up the original problem. Jourard says:

> Symptoms might be viewed as smokescreens interposed between the patient's real self and the gaze of the onlooker. We might call symptoms 'devices to avoid being known.'[75]

In his book *The Transparent Self* Jourard maintains that the tendency to keep secrets is the cause of many bodily ailments.[76] He continues:

> In the effort to avoid becoming known, a person provides for himself a cancerous kind of stress which is subtle and unrecognized, but nonetheless effective in producing not only the assorted patterns of unhealthy personality which psychiatry talks about, but also the wide array of physical ills that have come to be recognized as the province of psychosomatic medicine.[77]

In this Jourard is merely restating what King David told us:

> When I kept silence, my bones waxed old through my roaring all the day long. For day and night thy hand was heavy upon me: my moisture is turned into the drought of summer (Ps. 32:3, 4).

There seems to be broad agreement among psychiatrists and theologians that openness or confession to significant others does start one on the road to emotional peace. Many would agree with Drakeford when he says, "A man is never stronger than when he is admitting weakness."[78]

Jess Lair speaks of another dividend that comes from opening oneself up to others:

> Do this if you want to have more meaningful, closer relationships with others. All you need to do is with five people speak of what you feel in your deepest heart. Speak of these difficulties you have of accepting yourself. Speak of your fears and your worries. And you know what the other person is going to do? . . . Most of the five will want to be closer to you and they will reciprocate with the same thing. They will recognize their kinship with you. And they'll feel calm because they will see that you and they are in the same boat.[79]

It is more important, then, for man to find divine acceptance, the acceptance of others and self-acceptance through confession and forgiveness, as set forth by Drakeford, than to try in his own strength and intelligence to act more responsibly, as taught by Glasser.

We have seen that it is vitally necessary to discover and then evaluate the psychological presuppositions that underlie the various psychotherapies. If a counselor does not carefully evaluate his psychological presuppositions, he will be building upon an uncertain foundation.

6 Goals in Pastoral Counseling

The goals and values of the counselor have a great deal to do with those ultimately adopted by the counselee in the course of counseling. A pastor should not take the position of those counselors who believe they should not seek to influence the values or goals of their counselees.

The goals that will be discussed here not only have a definite Scriptural basis but also are those that a counselor with a heart of Christian concern would desire for those to whom he ministers.

A right relationship with God

The first goal in counseling the unsaved is to lead them to a saving knowledge of Jesus Christ. The only way for a man to be in a right relationship with God is through Jesus Christ and His redemptive work on the cross (John 14:6). The immediate consequences of redemption are relief from a guilty conscience and a sense of being accepted and loved by God.

When a man accepts the authority of the Word of God and has the Holy Spirit in his life, he is more likely to experience the emotional help he seeks. A right relationship with God is the first step to a right relationship with other men, for the new believer will be encouraged to see his problems in the light of God's Word.

The first goal in counseling one who is already a Christian is to encourage him to be in fellowship with the Lord and submissive in his attitude. There is not likely to be much progress in counseling a believer who has a stubborn inclination to do wrong and an equally stubborn unwillingness to admit to being wrong. Repentance and confession are vital factors in the restoration of a believer's fellowship with the Lord (1 John 1:9).

Spirit-controlled living

The pastor should seek to encourage believers to surrender their lives to the control of the Holy Spirit instead of allowing their old carnal natures to have dominance. He should show troubled believers the consequences of both carnal and spiritual living. He should seek to show relationships between carnality and particular psychological problems. It will be necessary to instruct carnal believers concerning Christian growth so that they may become more mature and more conformed to the image of Christ, and thus realize their own fullest potential and personal joy.

The counselee needs to see that the fruit of the Spirit (Gal. 5:22, 23) produces a life in conformity with the image of Christ. One of the chief characteristics of emotional and spiritual maturity is patience. He needs to learn gradually to be less childish and more adult, to insist less on immediately satisfying goal-responses and to put up with tensions necessary to achieve long-term goals.[1]

Enabled to deal decisively with the past

Some come into counseling with a great burden of guilt which needs to be relieved through the ministry of the Word of God. Others come with a great deal of resentment and bitterness which they need to allow the Holy Spirit to replace with mercy and forgiveness. Sometimes a better understanding of the other person's viewpoint can lessen hostility.

Some people did not get what they wanted from their parents when they were children, so they refuse to grow up until someone meets their needs. These people need to see that the past is past and that nothing can be done to undo it. They need to be shown that they are responsible for keeping the past alive in the present, and they must be taught to live rationally and maturely as Christians in the present. Dealing decisively with the past is often vital to progress in emotional healing.

Alleviation of distress

True healing should relieve the hurts that lie deeply buried in the psyche. "It is not difficult," says Branden,

> to establish that the average person carries within him the burden of an enormous quantity of unacknowledged and undischarged pain—not only pain originating in the present, but pain originating in the early years of his life.[2]

People need relief from intense and persistent fear, restlessness and anxiety. This anxiety at times is so intense that it entraps a person—rendering him unable to make important decisions.

Development of adequate self-esteem

The way a person sees himself and feels about himself is one of the greatest determinants of his behavior. A healthy self-concept is vital to psychological health, and a poor self-concept is at the root of much emotional distress and anti social behavior. Cain's low self-esteem was involved in the murder of his brother Abel. When self-esteem is low, a person is more likely to misinterpret another's attitude toward him—"He can't possibly think well of me."

When a person feels unlovable because he thinks there is something wrong with him, he will often hide himself instead of opening himself up to others. By hiding himself he cuts himself off from the love and affection from others that he really needs.

The Christian view of adequate self-esteem does not mean simply accepting ourselves just as we are. Our sinful natures and actions have caused us to think poorly of ourselves. An adequate and healthy and yet realistic self-esteem can come to us only by the grace of God. (Please see pages 55, 56.)

Acceptance of responsibility

Evasion of responsibility aggravates an emotional problem or delays its solution. The counselee is not taught *to assume* responsibility for his own life but rather *to recognize* the responsibility he already has. Branden has pointed out that assuming responsibility for one's life may be true in the realm of the financial or material, but that this is not man's option in relation to his psychological state. He says:

> On the psychological level, man does not have this option; by his nature, he is necessarily self-responsible; his option is only whether or not he will choose to be aware of the fact and to accept its consequences.[3]

In this instance, Adams, Drakeford, Glasser and Ellis would all agree with Branden. Freud's position, however, certainly lends itself to the unhealthy practice of blaming others, especially parents, for one's psychological problems.

Recognition of reality

The person who needs therapy is generally the one who has many misperceptions of himself and the world, which affect the way he feels and acts. A primary goal in counseling, then, is the development of a new method of thinking about the overlooked and obvious things about one's life and the world as it really is. It is also important that emotionally distressed persons increase their awareness of the repressions that may be of a defensive and disruptive nature. They need to be aware of all the forces, facts and fancies that influence their lives. They need to be aware of interpersonal and environmental factors, of spiritual and philosophical factors, and of their own wants, feelings and capacities

Since mental disorder is the result of the distortion between the way a person sees himself and other people, and the way they actually are, the recognition of reality is the precondition for alleviating emotional distress.

Integration of personality

An important goal in counseling is to bring about a wholeness or an integration of all the facets of one's being—mental, emotional, physical, spiritual, sexual and social—so the individual can be himself fully, naturally and simply. The goal is free-flowing, open and natural feelings and behavior; a life free from inner conflict and hypocrisy. Branden states the importance of integration:

> If it is true that his life depends upon his ability to think, then

it is equally true to say that his effective functioning as an organism, the fulfillment and enjoyment of his life, depends on the successful integration of thought, feelings and action. When that integration is broken—when thoughts, feeling and action are split off from one another, to operate in separate vacuums, so to speak—the result is disaster to the organism. One of the forms of that disaster is an impoverished sense of self.[4]

The average person gets his thinking, feelings and acting fragmented. It is common practice for a person to act one way on the outside and to think and feel another way on the inside, which is a form of insanity. Sometimes there is a conflict between reason and emotion—the reason pointing in one direction and the emotions in another. And sometimes an individual may have two conflicting emotions at the same time.

These inner conflicts or splits are sometimes handled consciously. For example, a conflict of feeling and action becomes so painful that the person determines he will never again do something that he does not deeply believe in. But when the conflict becomes too painful and the solution too difficult, repression often takes place. The result is self-defeating behavior patterns and a complete unawareness of one's lack of inner freedom and integrity. Counseling tries to put the person in touch with that part of the personality that has been lost or split off because of repression and to bring about a conscious reconciliation of the various aspects of his personality.

Nowhere is the matter of personality integration more important than in the matter of morals. Jesus Christ looked behind the deeds to the spirit in which they were done. In commenting on "moralism," Roberts sets forth clearly and fully the relationship between morals and integration:

It assumes that man can live up to any ideal or law that is obligatory upon him. He fulfills what he ought to do by making the principles of reason and conscience triumph over the irrational and sensuous elements in his makeup. Psychotherapeutic findings indicate, however, that this sort of organization of the self is not "free" at all. . . . It represents a continual condition of internal division and strife. The moralistic individual has not made fully "his own" the ideals which he strives to promote, and they fail to satisfy important needs and capacities. The more he has to force himself to conscientious effort, the more something in him is obviously resisting. The attempt to become virtuous *against* one's "wants" instead of by transformation of them is foredoomed to failure, and the history of moralism illustrates the failure. Ethical standards are insecure so long as they can be enforced only through coercion and conflict-ridden conscientiousness. Resistance to them gathers momentum, underneath the surface; and the more pressure is exerted to hold resistances in check, the more explosive and disruptive is their rebellion whenever they find an opportunity to break loose.[5]

The aim of parents, church leaders and school authorities should be that their young people willingly adopt their standards because of submission to the Scriptures, personal convictions and love for God. Only then will the young people follow the standards willingly and retain them into adulthood. Without this voluntary acceptance, the individual is likely to experience some degree of self-alienation and emotional distress.

Improve interpersonal relations

Another goal of counseling involves helping the individual to find freedom from interpersonal conflicts so that he can function smoothly in his relationship with others. It was Sullivan's major thesis that "the primary concern of psychiatry is the study of interpersonal relations."[6] Sullivan believed that most psychological problems arise in relation to the pursuit of security, which he defined as a state of well being, of belonging, of being accepted. His goal was to help people see the parataxic distortions that keep them from making secure and satisfying interpersonal relationships. By parataxic distortions he meant any attitude toward another person based on fantasy, or identification of that person with other figures,[7] or in Freudian language, "transference." As a result of their experience of anxiety in childhood, Sullivan believed that distressed individuals have a highly distorted view of themselves and of their relationships with others. Even though we may not agree with Sullivan that interpersonal relationships should be the major concern of our counseling, we will have to admit that, from both our own observations and our study of the Scriptures, interpersonal relationships are a vital factor in many mental and spiritual problems.

Help counselees willingly embrace Christian goals and values

Herein lies one of the greatest differences between Christian and secular counseling. Secular counselors, and even many religious counselors, tend to be relativistic in their moral positions; therefore, they are concerned only that individuals establish their own goals and values. But for the pastor-counselor to settle for this is to fail his Lord.

The significance of values for an individual's life is well expressed by Liebman:

> Meaning concerns having the belief that something counts, that there is something worth being here for; and that achievement of that something or the experience of that something, is purposeful and useful. It implies there is value and that living this value is meaningful through the two-fold process of expression and fulfillment.[8]

Counselors need to be aware that intentionally or unintentionally all psychotherapy or counseling involves a "decoding and recoding of the person's life code."[9]

Drakeford presents some of the suggestions that Freudian therapists have given that relate to values:

> Modify inappropriate superego controls, so that the patient can with less conflict and anxiety . . . successfully pursue erotic goals. The superego is modified and its severity reduced. Liberate the individual as completely as possible from anachronistic values, attitudes, strivings and defenses.[10]

Ellis speaks of

> The goal of finally getting the client to internalize a rational philosophy of living, just as he originally internalized the irrational ideas and attitudes of his parents, siblings, peer group, and the general culture.[11]

The clear implication of Ellis's goal is that the beliefs and values of parents, etc., are irrational and those of the therapist are rational. I am not denying that this may be the case occasionally, but Ellis certainly is not justified in making such a generalization. How vital it is, then, that the Christian counselor brings Biblical morality into his counseling.

It is generally recognized among therapists that counseling is a means by which individuals who have a poorly functioning value system are able to learn a new value system and to live more successfully because of it. The support of an apparently strong and successful person (counselor) in learning the new value system is of great benefit. It can be easily seen that a vibrant and spiritual counselor would have a great influence upon such individuals.

Since true morality must come from inner and freely willed value judgments, it is imperative that the counselees be regenerated by and submissive to the Spirit of God if they are to willingly embrace the values and goals of Christianity. Failure to willingly adopt Biblical values and goals is likely to result in both inward and outward conflict. Adoption of these values and goals is the way to inner peace and contentment.

The goals set forth in this chapter are either identical to or clearly in sympathy with those that any godly and concerned pastor would have for his people. They are realistic goals that may be reached by the grace of God.

7 Uncovering Techniques in Pastoral Counseling

Since one of the basic aims of counseling is self-knowledge, it is imperative to become aware of the many ways in which a person reveals what is deeply repressed in the unconscious. The methods used by the counselor to recover this material are called uncovering techniques. They are basic to diagnosing the nature of psychological disorders. Without uncovering the real problems, it is not likely that proper solutions will be offered. Jackson says, "One cannot be a successful counselor without studying diagnosis."[1]

While Rational Self-Analyses (which are taught in the last chapter) are a very effective means of uncovering, it is believed that they do not always uncover sufficiently. In some cases other uncovering techniques should be employed as well.

Psychological testing

Psychologists have developed tests that can help counselors to classify a person's problems, tell how he tries to adjust to life and show whether his perception (way of seeing things) or actions are interfered with by emotions or brain damage.[2] Such tests may reveal unconscious feelings that one may be unable to talk about. This information often greatly aids the counselor and shortens counseling time for the counselee.

Certain psychological tests are available only to ministers who are licensed by their state for this purpose; others like The Luscher Color Test can be purchased at any bookstore.[3]

Evaluation of the symptoms of emotional disorders Every symptom has a value to the counselee. The question needs to be asked, "What is the counselee getting out of the symptom?" While many symptoms are defensive in character, they also allow some indirect gratification of the repressed desire. White illustrates by the following case:

> A woman patient could go on the street only when accompanied by a relative; otherwise she was terrified that she would faint. It turned out that the street had a personal meaning of sexual temptation, being a place where she might get picked up by a man. Her phobia constituted a defense against this danger, but if she went out accompanied by a relative she could safely enjoy erotic fantasies whenever an attractive man passed by.[4]

A wife's aggressiveness toward her husband may be the result of her having done something wrong toward him. A man suspecting his wife of unfaithfulness may be paying for his own unfaithfulness to her. Scrupulosity is often found in individuals who really have something significant to feel guilty about.

Verbalizing

The term "verbalizing" refers to the counselor's or counselee's use of words in communicating with each other.

Some patients gain perspective about their emotions from just talking about them. They sometimes get a better view of their problems by having to explain them clearly to the counselor. Asking the counselee to write down in one small paragraph what the problem is has sometimes been very helpful in clarifying the issues.

Another use of verbalizing is to ask the counselee to describe in a noncritical manner the emotion he is feeling and to relate where in his body he is experiencing it and how exactly it feels to him. This helps him to acknowledge his undesired feelings and facilitate the process of healing integration by bringing his emotion into contact with his intelligence.[5]

When the pastor-counselor verbalizes by rephrasing what the counselee has been saying about his inner experience, it gives the counselee the assurance that the pastor is trying to help and understand him. It also helps the counselee to hear and see more clearly just what is taking place inside him.

Verbalizing may also take the form of giving or receiving feedback. The term "feedback" refers to letting others know how their behavior is affecting him or to learn from others how his behavior is affecting them.[6]

Probing

While it is contrary to client-centered practice to ask questions or to probe, it must not be assumed that it is improper for a pastor-counselor to do so. It is important to obtain a good understanding of the counselee's own views of his problem. For instance, the counselor may ask the counselee, "What good things do you see in your mate?" or "Would you try to describe for me your feelings of anger—to tell me where in your body you experience it and exactly how it feels to you?" Probing questions, when timed wisely, may help a person gain a fully-rounded picture of his situation, helping him to explore neglected aspects of his problem and to look for new solutions.

Surely the pastor cannot serve as a reliable guide unless he has all the information that is pertinent to the situation. Probing questions are usually the quickest and best way of obtaining that information.

Body language

The field of psychosomatic medicine has shown us the relationship between somatic processes and psychological phenomena. Because of this relationship, it is believed that man expresses himself in bodily movements, in posture, in pose, in expression and in gestures much more clearly than in words.

It has been observed that people often suck in and hold their breath and pull in and tighten their abdominal muscles when facing frightening, painful or anxiety producing situations. The muscle tension resulting from fear and anxiety manifests itself in various ways in the body. A counselor trained to observe these bodily manifestations will be aided considerably in making diagnoses.

The counselor should pay attention not only to what is being said but *how* it is being said. He will observe rate of speech, intonation, volume of speech, changes in volume, bodily posture, facial expressions, eye contact or lack of it, ease of speaking, biting nails, excessive smoking, facial tics, foot-tapping, finger drumming and whether or not the person sits calmly or squirms. It is believed that a person telling a story rather flatly but squirming while telling it is telling only part of the story.[7]

The counselor should be especially mindful of the various manifestations of rigidity—a stiff jaw, a stiff neck or a rather stiff walk.

Edward Cole explained how he gains information about the attitudes of a husband and wife who come for marital counseling by what they do with the chairs that he has strategically placed in front of his desk, fairly close together and turned somewhat inward toward each other. If the chairs are straightened or moved more widely apart by one of them, it reveals coolness on his part. The direction a person leans in his or her chair gives some indication of how one person is responding to the other.[8]

Study impulsive reaction

When an action is taken by a person impulsively that is in conflict with his conscious values, it is still an action which he has performed and expresses something important about his state at the time of performing it.[9]

A person may learn much about himself by "catching himself in the act." When a person catches himself in an unexpected response, he must not disown the response but ask what he can learn about himself from it. Impulsive reactions of anger, jealousy, dishonesty, etc., often tell people things about themselves of which they are not normally aware.

Exaggerated responses

Exaggerated responses show what is bothering us deep down. Incidents that could be expected to result in merely mild displeasure often bring about a burst of violent temper. Friendliness and a few smiles between a man and woman can sometimes result in a burning jealousy in a mate. A failure to notice someone can result in great feelings of rejection. Each of these exaggerated responses is clearly indicative of deep emotional problems.

Fantasy

Fantasy is the process of imagining objects or events in terms of imagery. It takes the form of both day and night dreaming.[10] Much of the content of daydreams makes us feel embarrassed. Daydreams are full of hurt feelings, petty, spiteful retaliation or absurdly glorious roles.

Most people will readily admit at least to themselves that their daydreams and fantasies reflect personal tendencies and reveal things of importance concerning their private worlds.[11]

Evaluation of wit and humor

Wit and humor offer the individual a way to express unconscious wishes. These wishes are often of a sexual or aggressive nature, as a critical examination of the jokes of our culture will reveal.

Evaluation of dreams

A single dream may yield key insights concerning a counselee's problem. Freud warned against dream interpretation that was not based on specific knowledge of a particular patient's unconscious conflicts. He insisted that a dream was always a wish fulfillment and therefore a royal route to the unconscious.[12]

Dreams may be regarded as spontaneous free associations and are of value because they allow feelings and attitudes to leak into awareness faster than might otherwise be the case.[13] It is believed that a careful analysis of dreams will show that they are somehow related to some aspect of one's conscious life and give some clue as to present inner conflicts.

Sentence completion

This is a technique whereby the counselor uses a list of phrases (the beginning of sentences) and asks the counselee to finish them with the first words that enter his mind. When a response is given that he wishes to explore further, other phrases are improvised which will bring out illuminating material.[14]

Some examples of the phrases used are: "I get angry when . . .", "I am hurt that . . .", "When I wake up in the morning. . . ."[15] The procedure for preparing the counselee is described by Branden as follows:

> I will say the first part of a series of incomplete sentences. As quickly and spontaneously as possible, you will reply with the first grammatical completion of the sentence that occurs to you. Try to avoid editing, censoring, or worrying about the rightness or appropriateness of your response. There are no "right" or "wrong" completions. We're simply interested in the first response that occurs to you. Never mind if the responses sound foolish, illogical, ridiculous or to the exact opposite of your beliefs. I suggest that you make yourself comfortable, let your hands rest at your sides, close your eyes, take a deep breath and let your body relax. Don't try to make anything happen. Don't try to analyze. Just let what happens happen of its own accord.[16]

The advantage of the sentence completion method is that it easily recovers repressed material which is of obvious significance to both the counselor and the counselee.

Imaginary conversations

An experiment described by Branden well illustrates this technique. He told his volunteer to sit in his chair, to relax, to let his arms rest at his sides, to close his eyes. Then he said:

> Now, . . . I want you to accept the following situation. You are lying on a hospital bed and you are dying. You are your present age. You are not in physical pain, but you are aware of the fact that in a few hours your life will end. Now, in your imagination, look up and see your mother standing at the side of the bed. Look at her face. There is so much unsaid between you—all the things

that you have never told her, all the thoughts and feelings you have never expressed. If ever you would be able to reach your mother, it is now. If ever she would hear you, it is now. Talk to her. Tell her. While I was speaking, the young man's hands clenched, blood rushed to his face, and one could see the muscular tension around his eyes and forehead that was aimed at repressing tears. When he spoke, it was a younger voice and much more intense, and his words were a rising moan as he said, "When I spoke to you, *why didn't you listen? . . . Why didn't you ever listen?*"[17]

Branden believed that there was a possible relationship between the frustration of a subject's need to be listened to as a child and his overly-reserved nature as an adult.

It is suggested that a person confront both of his parents one after the other in the above described manner. It is also suggested that the person imagine ideal parents and ask them for whatever he wants. This method is a way of getting a person in touch with his early frustrated needs which have been denied or repressed.

Prayer

A newly converted New York psychiatrist, Dr. Calabrese, tells of a woman client who had a terrible marital problem. She suffered from horrible nightmares and would wake up trying to say a particular word—"m m m m m"—and sometimes thrash around so that she fell out of bed. When none of his uncovering techniques worked, Dr. Calabrese asked if he could pray for her, asking the Lord to help her recall the repressed material. Upon her assent, he prayed for her, placing his hands upon her head. (It is to be noted that King David asked the Lord to reveal to him any repressed sinful material, Psalm 139:23, 24.) That night the lady had a dream in which she saw herself calling out, "Jesus, Jesus, Jesus." Then she saw Jesus open a closet door and her third-grade books fell out of it. These were the books that she had used when she was eight years old. She turned to Jesus in the dream and cried out, "Mmm-m-mother, Mother, Mother."

When she awakened at that point, she remembered that at the age of eight her drunken father had stumbled into her room one night and raped her. In her terror she had tried to call her mother and could not get a word out. Remembering this terrible experience opened up many other memories from her early life.[18]

Rational Self-Analysis

When a counselee involves himself in helping to solve his problem by doing a Rational Self-Analysis and going over it with his counselor, it is not unusual for previously unconscious material to come to consciousness.

Some of the suggested uncovering techniques are very much a part of the Rational Behavior Therapy method. Other of these techniques are helpful in giving insight to either the counselor or the counselee and may be used to suggest a subject for a Rational Self-Analysis. These other techniques may be readily employed by the counselor along with the RBT method.

8 Therapeutic Approaches in Pastoral Counseling

There is a growing trend toward employing a flexible repertoire of therapeutic approaches instead of being limited to one solitary approach. It is not necessary to make a hard and fast decision about whether to be passive or directive or something in between these two extremes. The counselor may determine it best to follow different roles when dealing with different kinds of issues. It is probably best to shift back and forth from the directive to the nondirective approach. No approach, however, will be very satisfying to the counselor or helpful to the counselee unless the counselor feels sincere and natural in using it.

Evangelism

Explaining the gospel of Jesus Christ and urging counselees to accept the Lord through faith and repentance will lay the groundwork for further progress in counseling. When the counselee comes to know Christ, he will have a hunger for the Word of God which will begin to renew his thinking (Rom. 12:2). Knowing Jesus Christ will also give him a greater ability to understand the Scriptures (1 Cor. 2:14). The sanctifying work of the Holy Spirit will do much to change irrational thinking and bruised emotions.

Admonition

There is absolutely no doubt about the Scriptural basis for admonition, for it is found throughout the Bible. Believers are admonished to love others, to forgive them, to say no to the world, the flesh and the devil, and to say yes to the Spirit of God.

Rollo May would argue that personality is not changed by advice.[1] But the Word of God is not merely advice; it is the power of God and the Sword of the Spirit, and it does have the power to change men. Men are not changed by an act of their own will in obedience to divine admonition but by the power of God in response to their faith and repentance.

Sometimes admonition may take the form of confrontation. The Scriptures do not support the kind of confrontation practiced in some group therapies—a kind of hostile confrontation expressing itself in a continuous attack using gut level language. But the Scriptures do support the kind of confrontation employed by Nathan, the prophet, with David (2 Sam. 12). Nathan told David the straight truth about himself, but it was done with a heart of love and in an attitude of respect.

Even some secular psychologists believe that strong positive suggestions can change irrational behavior and that less rational and less reality-oriented persons can learn more realistic ways of handling life's problems from more rational and reality-oriented people.[2]

In applying the Word of God to any situation, we need to be mindful of the warning given us by Dr. Martyn Lloyd-Jones in his book *Conversions Psychological or Spiritual:*

Another important principle is that in presenting the Christian gospel, we must never, in the first place, make a direct approach either to the emotions or the will. The emotions and the will should always be influenced through the mind. Truth is intended to come to the mind. The normal course is for the emotions and the will to be affected by the truth after it has first entered and gripped the mind. It seems to me that this is a principle of Holy Scripture. . . . We are to plead with men, but never to bring pressure . . . we are never to browbeat. This, it seems to me, is a vital distinction which every preacher and missioner must always bear in mind.[3]

Love

Authentic love involves sacrifice and commitment. When a counselor loves a counselee, the counselor will do all in his power to alleviate the counselee's emotional distress and help make his life more meaningful. Love will express itself in empathy and positive regard. The counselor will have a positive regard for the individual even though there may be some things about him that he does not like at all.

Calabrese tries to find something attractive about the counselee and focuses upon it. If he can't find an element of attractiveness in him, he does not even try to work with him.[4] When the counselor really cares about someone, it will show in his behavior. The individual will get the message that the counselor really wants him to be helped.

Love provides a kind of relationship and atmosphere in which the person no longer needs his old defenses. Once the emotional blocks are dissolved, the cognitive aspects of the personality can function more adequately. When the person becomes free to feel and to see and to acknowledge all that he truly is, changes are likely to occur.

By emphasizing the love of God for the counselee, the counselor helps him regain his self-esteem. He begins to realize that the most significant Person loves him. The regaining of self-esteem will have far-reaching consequences in every area of his life.

Besides the love of the counselor and God, the person may need the warm and loving fellowship of a church family. Self-esteem once regained must be sustained through social reinforcements.[5]

Honesty

Jeremiah 17:9 says, "The heart is deceitful . . ." and David said, "Behold, thou desirest truth in the inward parts" (Ps. 51:6). Since lying to oneself is at the root of emotional disorder, it becomes evident that basic honesty is a necessity if the problem is to be solved. Even such serious disorders as schizophrenia are considered by some psychologists to originate in a break with sincerity. The large amount of damage done to the schizophrenic's self-esteem is believed to result from his "contemplation of his own vicious insincerity."[6]

Repression, the primary defense mechanism, is seen as a form of evasion, which because of its very nature is an anti-integration process. One of the counselor's chief responsibilities is to point out the self-deceptive tendencies to the counselee and to encourage him to discontinue concealing the shortcomings of the past. He is to be encouraged to let others know how he feels in his deepest heart.

Repentance

Repentance (a change of mind) is being more and more recognized by psychologists as a necessary element in the process of restoring one to a state of emotional well-being. Repentance is a prerequisite to changing one's behavior. It was because the prodigal son changed his mind about his sin, his friends, his father, his predicament, life back home and about himself that he decided to go back home to his father.

Unsaved counselees need to be encouraged to repent (Luke 13:5). Believers, too, often have a need of repentance in relation to some aspect of their lives.

Confession

Emotionally ill people are typically guilty people. Guilt is a state of anxiety due to either self-hatred or a loss of self-esteem.

Confession to God involves being honest with oneself and with a significant other. Forgiveness is often not fully experienced without confessing to another human being as well as to God. Confession often involves the psychological processes of both abreaction and emotional catharsis.[7]

Abreaction involves the discharge of tension by reliving an unpleasant experience in one's mind and emotions.

When we "feel" the greatness or seriousness of our sin against another as David did after being confronted by Nathan, we are more likely to be honest and open with our confession. And when we honestly feel our hurt and resentment toward others who have offended us, we are able to more honestly deal with them and seek the Lord's help to put away our bitterness. No longer are the sinful feelings repressed—they are faced fully and realistically.

Multitudes of Christians can testify that their guilty memories have entirely disappeared after confessing their sins to God. Like David, they experienced the blessedness of the man whose sins are covered (Ps. 32:1).

Forgiving others

The individual who feels that he has been denied love and acceptance is often pessimistic and has a demanding attitude towards life. He may think that because he was not given what he wanted, he will not give others what they want. He is filled with resentment.

Often a person's resentment is toward a parent. Sometimes this resentment can be lessened by getting him to ask what his grandparents were like. He will usually better understand his own parent then, and this understanding often results in forgiveness.

Even when forgiveness cannot be encouraged through sympathetic understanding, it is imperative that all bitterness and resentment be put away (Eph. 4:31), for it can only bring emotional pain and distress to the one who harbors it.

Hope

Hope and trust are the psychological characteristics of emotional well-being. Anything a counselor does that encourages the distressed person to have hope that a better life is possible has therapeutic value.

Basil Jackson states:

> Man's only sense of meaning, purpose and reason for existence appears to be not in the past or present but in the future. In fact, there is no such thing as the present for as immediately as it arrives, it is already in the past tense. . . . If hope is not applied to man, he will shrivel up and die in the void of purposeless activity. . . .

If one is to hope, he must believe in his ability to change the status quo and to transcend the present situation.[8]

Since the chief psychological component of Christianity is hope, the pastor is often able to help when other counselors fail. The believing pastor can, as an ambassador of Christ, offer people the hope of forgiveness, of victory over sin, of grace sufficient, of an abundant life and of a glorious eternity.

Humility

Humility is a vital prerequisite for finding relief from emotional distress. Humility is not a feeling of inferiority or self-hatred or an attitude of passivity but an honest and heartfelt sense of needing God. It is admitting to oneself and to God that he cannot work his way out of his problem without God. It involves crying out to God to make him what he would like to become, a person of worth to himself and to the world in which he lives.

A distressed person often needs to recognize that pride, the opposite of humility, has selfishness as its root. When such individuals humble themselves, emotional healing often takes place. Here the Christian message and Christian grace can accomplish what secular therapy cannot do.

Assuming responsibilities

Emotionally distressed people need to be convinced that part of the price of human existence is the process of becoming accountable. They are accountable to parents, to teachers, to spouses, to courts, to police and to God. They need to understand that evasion of responsibility aggravates a problem or delays its solution. When a person accepts responsibility for what he is, change can be expected.

Assuming responsibility involves looking at our own faults and no one else's. We can do something about our own faults but can do little about the faults of others. Often one has to take full blame to himself when he begins to see that the people he has previously blamed are no longer around. A person must be led to see that his present condition is the logical result of his past behavior.

Blaming others also has the effect of blocking off major sources of self-esteem found in positive relationships with others; one cannot be rightly related to another whom he is constantly blaming. Christianity emphasizes personal responsibility for sin and the means of its forgiveness. It also enables man to do something about the problems he was previously unable to solve.

Finding meaning

The primary difficulty of some people is related to finding the meaning of life. According to Frankl, the originator of Logo-therapy, "the striving to find a meaning in one's life is the primary motivational force to man."[9] Man needs something for which to live. By giving special emphasis to the meaning in one's life, the focus of the counseling is on the future rather than the past. Focusing on the future also helps to break up the self-centeredness which is so typical of the emotionally distressed individual.

The pastor-counselor will find that talking about meaning in life will offer a wonderful opportunity to share the truths of the gospel with the unconverted. When dealing with believers, he should stress the fact that they must make the best of their lives; they must not waste their lives in sin or on trifles. They must be encouraged to live for a purpose of which they will not be ashamed on their deathbeds or at the Judgment Seat of Christ.

Decision making

Since most emotional problems are rooted in the personal choices that individuals make daily, one of the counselor's main tasks is to help people make more rational choices. One of the most important decisions is to change oneself. Some people admit that conquering their problems is not so much the result of understanding the causes or of miraculously losing the tendency to do something; it is the result of *deciding* to ignore the memories of failure and of taking the necessary steps, gradually and persistently, toward a safer, more satisfying life.

It may be helpful to the distressed person to recall which life choice or decision is behind the present problem. He needs also to ask himself what "pay offs" or advantages he is receiving from the situation as it is. Not every counselee wants to be rid of his pain. Branden speaks of "an individual's willful alienation from the possibilities of his own growth—for the sake of clinging to a childhood irredeemably behind."[10] Soul-searching along these lines will be helpful in making decisions in the present.

A counselor may aid a counselee in making decisions by encouraging him to get all the available information possible within the available time. He should also encourage the counselee to consider all of the various alternatives open to him.

When discussing decision making in relation to changing oneself, there are two issues we must face:

1. There is an immense gap between the plan to change and the commitment to change. Commitment to change involves some definite and meaningful action in the direction of the planned change.

2. Man does have the power to make meaningful decisions. The Christian view of man, which stresses the centrality of the will and of responsible freedom, is much but not entirely in agreement with the views of many modern psychiatrists. The agreement lies in recognizing the experience of responsibility which we know as an essential part of human life. Wilson presents James's view that we "become aware of our free [sic] will when we are making an effort. For it is then that we become aware that we can increase or decrease the effort."[11] Branden's view of human volition is so strongly slanted toward "free will" as to deny the bondage to sin taught in the Bible. He states:

> As a being of volitional consciousness, a being who is psychologically free to think or not to think, to focus his conscious mind or to avoid the effort and responsibility of doing so, man can strive to expand the range of his awareness or he can, in effect, cooperate with his subconscious resistance to awareness—and thereby tacitly participate in the sabotaging of his mental health.[12]

We cannot agree with Hume or with some psychologists

who hold that acts of will or any kind of thoughts are the natural outcome of physical processes—simple reflexes. To these psychologists, thought is a mere association of ideas that is as mechanical as our physical reflexes.

As Christians, we are aware of some limits upon our freedom because of our selfish natures. We also recognize that God does not treat us as puppets but as responsible people who are able to make meaningful decisions. However, we cannot by our own act of will (a decision) free ourselves from our sin nature (John 8:34, 36) or change ourselves into something that is acceptable to God (Rom. 8:7, 8).

Acting responsibly

Glasser's major thesis is that emotionally distressed people are helped most when they are encouraged to act responsibly in meeting their own needs. Though I disagree with Glasser's almost total neglect of one's unconscious past, it is not necessary to disavow his counsel about acting responsibly in the present. The Scriptures would certainly substantiate this counsel, but at the same time they do not ignore the effects of unconscious habits of thinking.

By acting responsibly (in accordance with Scripture) today, the counselee is certainly going to have less to trouble his soul tomorrow (Prov. 13:15; Isa. 57:20, 21).

Restitution

Drakeford's Integrity Therapy, which stresses mainly the volitional level of life, emphasizes the importance of restitution. Besides the clear Scriptural support for restitution (Num. 5:6, 7; Matt. 5:23, 24; Luke 19:8) there also seems to be a firm psychological basis for it. Man seems to want a way of expiating or working off his guilt in some constructive way.

We who believe in the finished work of Christ on the cross need to guard against giving counselees the impression that they need to *do* something or *suffer* something in order to be forgiven. The conditions of forgiveness are trusting the sacrifice of Christ and repentance. A key question arises: Has a person truly repented of (changed his mind about) a sin that he has committed if he is not willing to do what he can to ameliorate the effects of his sin? It may take an act of restitution to convince the individual in his own mind that he has truly repented. Restitution is not necessary to being saved, but in some cases it may be necessary to feeling forgiven.

It is obvious that, in relation to some sins, nothing can be done to undo their harmful consequences, as in the case of David's sin against Uriah the Hittite. It is clear that David experienced the forgiveness of the Lord because he believed the Word of God by the prophet Nathan—"The Lord also hath put away thy sin" (2 Sam. 12:13)—even though he could not restore Uriah's life.

In the light of such a case as David's and of the Scriptural teaching concerning forgiveness, we should use great care in seeking to bring about emotional relief through restitution.

Identification with Jesus Christ

The pastor has the privilege of informing believers of their freedom from the bondage of sin because of their identification with Jesus Christ in His death (Rom. 6:6). Just as some slaves, after the Proclamation of Emancipation, continued doing the same work, getting the same pay, taking orders from the same people and feeling the same about their masters, so many believers continue their lives as though they are still in bondage to sin. Just as it took time for some of the slaves to recognize and act upon their freedom, so it takes time for many believers to recognize and act upon their spiritual freedom.

The death referred to must of necessity be a judicial death, not an actual one. The death is of the "old man," or the old Adamic life which is at enmity with God (Rom. 8:7) and is the source of sin (Gal. 5:19, 21). It was this old man (flesh nature, not body) that controlled our behavior.

When a person accepts Jesus Christ as his Savior, the death of Christ becomes effective for him. His sins and his sin nature have been judged already. The judgment of sins was a past event, but the experience of sins forgiven is a present one. Paul refers to this in the latter part of Romans 6:6 where he says, "that the body of sin might be destroyed." By the "body of sin" I believe Paul means that aspect of our physical lives that has been under the control of sin (we inherit sinful tendencies). The word "destroyed" means "rendered powerless." Paul apparently is telling us that when the judgment of our old sinful nature becomes effective for us (at conversion), the power of the old nature over us is broken. It still exists, it has not been eradicated and it can still influence us, but it can no longer control us. We no longer sin as slaves but as free men—voluntarily sinning.

The power of the sinful nature is broken by the presence of the Holy Spirit, Who is given to us at conversion (Acts 2:38; Gal. 5:16). The broken power of the sinful nature can also be seen by the fact that we are no longer under the law (Rom. 6:14). Paul explains in Romans 7:5 that "when we were in the flesh, the motions [passions] of sins, which were by the law, did work in our members to bring forth fruit unto death." Before conversion, when under the law, the law actually stirred up sinful passions. Now that we are under grace instead of law, we are no longer stirred up by it to sin. In fact, we are now married to a new Husband, Jesus Christ, instead of to the law, that we might serve in newness of spirit (Rom. 7:6).

Identification with Jesus Christ also involves our sharing in His resurrection power (Rom. 6:4; Eph. 1:19, 20; 2:5) and in our being seated with Him right now in heavenly places (Eph. 2:6). We are accepted in the beloved, we are heirs of God and joint heirs with Jesus Christ. Since we are "somebodies" now in the eyes of God, it should do something for our self-esteem, our appreciation of God's grace and our expectation of glory.

Surrender

Stubbornness or an unwillingness to change is one of the main reasons for the lack of positive results from counseling. Surrender to the standards and principles of God's Word will often produce dramatic results in the emotionally distressed person.

It is good to point out that one must not stop with one act of surrender. The crisis surrender must be followed by a process of surrender.

Patience

Having set realistic and Scriptural goals for themselves, counselees should be encouraged to give themselves plenty of time to change to some new and better way. They must be instructed not to give up on themselves because of failure or sin but to turn to the Lord in repentance and confession (1 John 1:9). They must be made to realize that being conformed to the image of Christ is a process, not something that is attained in a one-time crisis experience.

Faith

"Without faith it is impossible to please God" (Heb. 11:6). When a distressed person begins to see how the Word of God applies to his problem, it can have a dramatic effect upon his thinking, feeling and behavior. Faith in Christ's power to deliver from the bondage of sinful habits, and faith in His power to give an abundant life, have given many the hope they needed to start them on the path to emotional peace.

It is very impressive that every one of the therapeutic approaches set forth in this chapter has an explicit Biblical basis, though the chapter was not planned with this in mind. Approaches were included on the basis of their effectiveness.

9 Rational Behavior Therapy: an Effective Model for Pastoral Counseling

Rational Behavior Therapy (RBT), sometimes called Rational Emotive Therapy (RET), is a cognitive-emotive-behavioristic approach to emotional disorder expounded primarily by Albert Ellis and Maxie Maultsby, Jr. It is a very effective and yet easily learned technique for uncovering the irrational and distorted ideas that are at the root of emotional distress. It also offers a framework for employing any of the therapeutic approaches reviewed in the previous chapter.

A Bible-believing pastor cannot accept RBT in its entirety but is obliged, rather, to cull out, refine and add to it in order to bring it into accord with Scripture.

The humanistic bent of RBT is seen in its emphasis upon man's ability, without any help from God or the Scriptures, to straighten out his irrational thinking.[1]

In some instances it is true that, by reason alone, man can become aware of his former irrationality and begin to think rationally and to act responsibly. This accounts for the degree of success that RBT has enjoyed among unregenerate people. But straight thinking about some of the greatest issues of life such as the origin of man, the purpose of his existence, standards of behavior, and human responsibility is impossible without accepting the authority of the Word of God. Rational thinking apart from God may help solve some problems, but it cannot tell us of divine forgiveness and acceptance or deliver us from the misery, guilt, shame, despair or loneliness resulting from sinful behavior. Nor can it deliver us from the sufferings of hell. According to Jesus, it is better if a person were never born than to live and die in antagonism toward God (Matt. 26:24).

Rational Behavior Therapy also teaches a relativistic morality which is based on enlightened self-interest and individualism. Maultsby, in counseling a sexually promiscuous woman who was feeling bad about herself, advised her not to confuse herself with her behavior.[2] He later encouraged her to decide for herself whether or not her promiscuity was rational.[3] In a discussion with David Goodman he clearly promotes situation ethics as "the only guide consistently worked out that we can follow in human morality."[4] Evidently Maultsby does not think much of either the Ten Commandments or the Sermon on the Mount.

The main thesis of RBT is "that people can live the most self-fulfilling, creative and emotionally satisfying lives by disciplining their thinking."[5]

The aims of RBT are to alleviate emotional distress by overcoming self-defeating thinking habits of long standing, and to condition the mind to understand and apply rational thinking.

Type of approach

RBT is a highly directive method that uses strong confrontational methods in attacking the counselee's irrational ideas and tries to induce him to adopt more rational ones. While attacking his ideas, there is a positive regard for the person himself.

The nature of RBT clearly places it among those psychotherapies that follow the *educative* model rather than the *conditioning* or *medical* models. It provides much instruction concerning the nature of emotions, the irrationality of man, the tests of rationality and the means of behavior modification.

Though not generally considered a depth-centered psychotherapy, it may be argued that it is just that because it seeks to reveal and attack the irrational ideas, beliefs or values that underlie emotional disorder.

Instead of concentrating on such irrelevant ideas as the Oedipus complex or the pernicious influences of unloving parents, RBT focuses its attention on the present-day thinking that is causing the emotional disturbance. RBT theory rejects the idea that the original causes of an emotional disturbance can be accurately known; therefore, it stresses that prolonged analysis of the past is unnecessary.

RBT offers much flexibility, so it is not surprising to find in it the key insights of several other psychotherapies. It stresses reality and responsibility as does Glasser's Reality Therapy; it emphasizes the place of volition as does Drakeford's Integrity Therapy; it employs admonition as does Adams's Nouthetic Counseling; it uses a relaxation technique similar to Lowen's Bioenergetics and it teaches a kind of aversive-conditioning as Wolpe did. And because of this flexibility, a pastor may easily work into its framework those therapeutic approaches that have a Scriptural basis.

An unusual characteristic of RBT is its emphasis upon self-counseling. Because no method of counseling works unless the person who needs it puts it into action, the most effective counseling is self-counseling.

The approach of RBT may rightly be called a semantic approach. It is based upon the premise that all thinking depends upon the use of words. People's thinking, including their beliefs, attitudes, opinions and values, all take the form of internalized sentences or self-talk. People are constantly telling themselves various sane or crazy things which are reflected in their emotions and actions.

One of the most effective ways of changing people and their emotions is to teach them insight. They must clearly see and understand their internal verbalizations so as to dispute them according to rules of rationality and, if necessary, to alter them. RBT is not *just* semantic, it is *all* semantics. Thinking cannot take place without words. Close your eyes and try to communicate with yourself without the use of words. It is impossible. Your thoughts are essentially the same as your words.

We can alter our emotions by altering our words. We normally react logically to our own words. For example, you will feel differently if you:

1. Call a person careless instead of a stupid idiot.
2. Call a man black instead of a nigger.
3. Call a person a strong leader instead of a dictator.
4. Say it is very difficult to diet instead of it is impossible to diet.
5. Say that the boss saw you make a mistake and brought it to your attention instead of, "My boss chewed me out."

RBT's emphasis upon rationally understanding one's emotions has opened it to the criticism of being too cold, of blocking intense emotions. Ellis answers that reasoning does block inappropriate or self-defeating emotion, but that reasoning and appropriate emotion are compatible and that, in the long run, rational thinking leads to increased feelings of pleasure.[6]

Causes of irrationality

Ellis believes that some of man's illogical ideas are rooted in his genetic makeup. He is quoted by Gross as saying, "We are probably born with a constitutional, genetic tendency to be disturbed. In any case, it is usually impossible to find the origin of disturbance in our past history."[7] He believes, however, that most irrational ideas are derived from one's early upbringing and from the society in which one lives. Scripture agrees with RBT's view that there is an unusual tendency for human nature to pervert and distort the truth (Jer. 17:9).

Thinking according to RBT theory

Ellis, though not taking an absolutist position, holds that by the time we reach adulthood, practically all of us do most of our important thinking and consequently our emoting, "in terms of self-talk, or internalized sentences."[8]

Thinking, then, is a train of ideas manifesting itself in subvocal speech. Thinking itself is, Ellis states, "a relatively calm appraisal of a situation, an objective comparison of many of its elements, and a coming to some conclusion as a result of this comparing process."[9]

Maultsby holds that perceiving and thinking are learned behavior, and he therefore aims at teaching people how to perceive reality more realistically so as to increase their personal satisfaction in life.[10]

Although the main insight of RBT is that irrational thinking produces disaster in the emotional sphere, it is also recognized that a denial or repression of feeling results in disaster in the intellectual sphere. A good example of this is the person who carries much free-floating anger around with him and who, as a result, finds the world he encounters also to be angry in order to justify his own feelings of anger. Even in this case, where emotions have influenced thinking, it is evident that it is the thinking element in the original free-floating hostility that needs to be discovered and handled if the person is to live more effectively.

Branden clearly states the relationship of one's values to his thinking:

> In untangling the roots of his patient's problems, the therapist will find that he must constantly move back and forth between psycho-epistemological errors and emotional or motivational conflicts; i.e., between his patient's method of thinking and his mistaken values and premises. A relationship of reciprocal causation exists between the spheres of cognition and evaluation. Just as rational thinking encourages the formation of rational values, and the formation of rational values encourages rational thinking—so unhealthy thinking tends to result in unhealthy values, and unhealthy values tend to result in unhealthy thinking.[11]

It is also vital that we see the relationship between one's thinking and self-concept. Branden points out:

> A person's view and estimate of himself—his self-concept and self-evaluation are . . . the vital center of his psychology: They are the motor of his behavior. In attempting to understand his patient's problems and to help solve them, the psychotherapist must constantly relate psycho-epistemological and motivational (or emotional) disorders to the nature of the patient's self-esteem.

If, for example, a patient typically evades, represses, rationalizes in a certain area of his life—the therapist must ask: What purpose is served relative to the maintainence of the patient's self-esteem (or pseudo-self-esteem)?[12]

Emotions in RBT theory

The world is an orderly place in which things happen only when conditions for their happening have been met. Emotions, then, do not just mysteriously exist in their own right; they are caused.

Not only our perceptions but our evaluation of what we perceive causes our emotions. Human beings do not receive information by means of their senses and then automatically react; they evaluate the information and then react emotionally or behaviorally. Goodman points out that Epictetus, the ancient Greek philosopher, was unaware of this truth when he said, "Man is not disturbed by events, but by the view he takes of them."[13] As an illustration of this, picture yourself all alone in your house at night. You suddenly wake up to a strange tapping sound. As you listen to it, you think there is someone in the house. As you make your way down the hallway, you are very frightened. You go into the front room where the noise is coming from, and you realize that the sound is coming from an open window. The wind is moving the venetian blind against the window. You have a very different feeling now. Your gut feeling reversed itself. What happened? The objective reality did not change at all. The cause of the noise remained the same. How you interpreted the noise made the difference, and when you interpreted the facts correctly, your feelings changed. That is just what RBT is all about.

We also perceive our own thoughts and memories and evaluate them as well. This makes it possible to have emotional reactions to thoughts themselves. Emotion, then, is almost always caused and controlled by thinking.

Although emotions are primarily caused by thinking, they can be influenced by electric shock treatments, drugs, relaxation exercises, primal screaming or yoga breathing exercises. These methods are viewed not as cures but as means of merely temporary relief.

Human beings are thought to function holistically—perceiving, thinking, emoting and moving simultaneously. Each of these processes "significantly overlap and denote different aspects of the same life processes."[14] Thinking, then, involves not only evaluating and remembering but also sensory, motor and emotional behavior.

People do not go to counselors or to psychiatrists because their thoughts are irrational, but because they are hurting emotionally. Therefore, one of the counselor's first aims is to educate people concerning the origin of their emotions. Then he should show them the need to substitute more rational and realistic thinking for the self-defeating self-talk which is bringing them misery.

Emotions may be defined as value responses (something is good or bad) that involve a high level of activation, visceral and behavioral changes and strong feelings. The reason RBT attacks the thinking and evaluation aspects of emotion is because it is believed that thoroughgoing and permanent changes in one's disturbed emotions take place through the use of reason and reality-testing.

The approach to the unconscious in RBT is rather unique. It holds that the deeply unconscious thoughts or needs of most people are not really so deep. Instead of being in the unconscious, Ellis believes that such thoughts are merely preconscious—thoughts and feelings of which we are not immediately aware, but which can be easily brought to consciousness. One of Ellis's methods of bringing thoughts to consciousness is to learn to infer them by working back from the behavior (actions and emotions) that they induce. He goes on to explain how unconscious thoughts rise to consciousness:

> We firmly believe that, whatever your emotional upsets, you can learn to perceive the cerebral self-signaling that invariably lies behind and motivates your emotions—and thereby succeed in deciphering the "unconscious" messages you transmit to yourself.

Once you clearly see, understand, and begin to dispute the irrational beliefs that create your inappropriate feelings, your "unconscious" thoughts will rise to consciousness, greatly enhancing your power of emotional self-control.[15]

The main premise of RBT, then, is that a very large and important part of what we call emotion is the direct result of strongly evaluative thinking.

Maultsby's Rational Self-Analysis is structured upon his definition of a complete emotion as being composed of (a) your perception, (b) your evaluating thoughts and (c) your emotive feelings.[16] It must also be noted that the evaluations that the brain automatically makes are either positive, negative or relatively neutral. Emotions, then, are value judgments—and they are always logical, correct and appropriate to **how you are evaluating a situation.**

The brain in RBT theory

Your brain controls your emotional and physical reactions. But you direct your brain with your thoughts. Your brain can't tell if your thoughts are believable but irrational, or believable and rational. You have to do that. Your brain will use either type of thoughts with the same ease and speed in controlling your emotions and physical actions. Rational self-counseling makes your brain favor believable and rational thoughts.[17]

In the light of Maultsby's preceding explanation of the way the brain functions, the counselor must encourage people to question the validity of their sincerely held beliefs, attitudes and thoughts. His aim is also to help them make rational choices.

Our brains often control us by habits to which we have become enslaved. Habits are formed by our repeatedly choosing to do something. For example, when you habitually think the same types of thoughts about **your perception of** a particular extreme event, you will begin to automatically react to that type of perception with positive, negative or neutral feelings. Your emotional habits are being converted into relatively permanent personality traits and into relatively permanent attitudes or beliefs.

The two main parts of the brain are the neocortex or the thinking part of the brain, and the limbic or the feeling part of the brain. You notice and form images of yourself and the world with the neocortex. You also understand, start, maintain and stop your emotional and physical reactions by using your neocortex, but it does not force you to do any of these things in the most correct and rational manner. The neocortex treats mistaken thoughts as though they were factual, if you believe them. If you don't direct your brain carefully, it will make mental images using impulses from your memory and imagination without your realizing it.

Rules for rational thinking

Ellis and Maultsby offer five rules for testing the rationality of one's thinking.[18] When using them, the pastor-counselor may wish to add a few rules to include aspects of reality that are crucial to the Christian faith. We shall consider each of the five rules briefly:

1. It is based on objective reality.

"Reality," according to Basil Jackson, "is that which is consensually verifiable by others of the same mentality, and of the same educational and cultural background. It is consensually observable."[19] In doing Rational Self-Analysis objective reality is determined by a "camera check"; that is, anything that a camera could photograph or a tape recorder could pick up.

The objective is to remove from the picture to which one is reacting all subjective elements—the things he has put into the picture through his own imagination. By doing this, his thoughts, feelings and actions will be based only on what is really happening. He will be guarding against unwarranted assumptions and jumping to conclusions.

2. It protects your life.

Generally, this means that any action that seriously jeopardizes one's life is considered to be irrational. Examples would be drinking, smoking, overeating or playing "chicken" on the highway.

There are some exceptions, however, for the Christian who, like Paul, hazarded his life for the sake of the gospel of Christ.

3. It helps you achieve your goals.
Much thinking is actually self-defeating. Some students say to themselves, "I could never learn geometry or chemistry." A young man might say of a young lady whom he would like to date, "She will never go out with me." An example of rational thinking would be a man of average intelligence saying to himself, "If other men of my intelligence have been able to obtain their college degrees through night school, so can I."

4. It keeps you out of conflict with others.
Does your thinking on a particular issue keep you out of trouble or plunge you into it? God's Word teaches us "as much as lieth in you, live peaceably with all men" (Rom. 12:18). When no principle of Scripture is compromised by our giving in to the wishes of others in order to avoid conflict with them, it should be seriously considered as the course of action to take.

5. It eliminates significant emotional conflict.
As long as we are alive and conscious, there will be a conflict of motivation within our minds. If we are thinking rationally, we will not think those thoughts that bring us a degree of internal conflict that we are not willing to accept. The believer, for example, knows that letting the Holy Spirit control his life will involve him in a conflict with his old fleshly nature (Gal. 5:16, 17). Another example is a person who is willing to say no to his appetite in order to gain the satisfaction of looking slim. A rational person who wishes for riches is not willing to suffer the mental conflict and burden that results from being a bank robber.

I propose adding the following two rules so that rationality may be evaluated in the light of Christianity.

6. It is based upon spiritual realities.
A believer, or even an unbeliever, needs to take into his consideration the following spiritual realities (which could not be verified by the camera check): A holy God, Jesus Christ, the Holy Spirit, Heaven, hell, judgment to come and the love and grace of God.

7. It is based upon Scriptural principles.

Any thought, emotion or action that is contrary to the Word of God is spiritually irrational. Whether or not we can understand His ways (Isa. 55:8, 9), it pays to obey God's Word. How man needs to learn this lesson taught by Eve's first irrational act!

Almost the entire history of Israel bears witness that people are not rational when they disregard God's Word.

Common irrational ideas

The most common irrational ideas of our modern American culture are set forth by Ellis and Harper in their book *Guide to Rational Living*. These ideas are presented in summary form by Goodman. I have taken the liberty of excluding one idea (his #3), which could not be considered irrational by a Bible-believing Christian, and of adding some other irrational ideas.

Along with the list of irrational ideas, I have included some of my own comments and Scripture references which prove these ideas to be not only irrational but also unscriptural. The list follows:

1. It is a dire necessity for you to be loved or approved by almost everyone for virtually everything you do (Luke 6:26).

2. You should be thoroughly competent, adequate and achieving in all possible respects. Some think that if their performances are not nearly perfect, they are failures (Rom. 12:3–6; 1 Cor. 12:14–18).

3. It is terrible, horrible and catastrophic when things are not going the way you would like them to go (Rom. 8:28). You exaggerate the importance of things such as your mistakes or the achievements of other people. A single negative event is taken as a never-ending pattern of defeat. A single negative detail spoils everything.

4. Human unhappiness is externally caused and people have little or no ability to control their sorrows or rid themselves of their negative feelings (Phil. 3:1; 4:4).

5. If something is or may be dangerous or fearsome, you

should be terribly occupied with it and upset about it. Illustrations would be the possiblity of being unemployed or the fear of a nuclear holocaust (Phil. 4:6, 7).

6. It is easier to avoid facing many of life's difficulties and self-responsibilities than to undertake some rewarding forms of self-discipline (Gal. 6:5; Phil. 4:13).

7. The past is all-important and because something once strongly affected your life, it should indefinitely do so (Phil. 3:13).

8. People and things should be different from the way they are (Rom. 3:10; 8:7; 2 Tim. 3:1–4), and it is catastrophic if perfect solutions to the grim realities of life are not immediately found.

9. Maximum human happiness can be achieved by inertia and inaction, or by passively and uncommittedly enjoying yourself (John 15:10, 11).[20]

10. Positive experiences don't count when you already have a negative belief (Exod. 16:3).

11. You feel it, therefore it must be true (1 Kings 19:10).

12. You can read people's minds. This is the basis for jumping to conclusions (2 Kings 5:11).

13. You can foretell the future. This is the basis for worry (Prov. 27:1).

14. By mislabeling something or someone with language that is highly colored and emotionally loaded, you can actually change your evaluation of reality to be what you label it (1 Sam. 15:13, 20).

Characteristics of irrational thinkers

Goodman's list of the characteristics of irrational thinkers is very helpful to anyone who wishes to evaluate his own thinking or the thinking of others. The characteristics are as follows:

1. High degree of interpersonal difficulties.

2. Persistence of emotionalism in reacting to daily problems.

3. Desiring what one cannot have or is unlikely to get.

4. Not wanting or appreciating what one has or could get.

5. Tendency to attribute all one's difficulties to others.

6. Tendency to see oneself as worthless.

7. Pursuit of contradictory goals, or behavior that is inconsistent with professed goals.

8. Tolerating bad situations rather than taking steps to rectify or improve them.

9. Prejudice against individuals as members of a group.

10. Hypersensitivity to criticism.

11. Using means that are antiethical to the goals sought.

12. Remaining dependent on others past the necessary period.

13. Being angry or hurt past a reasonable period of time.

14. Inability to tolerate uncertainity.

15. Demand for perfection in one's own behavior or in that of others.

16. Demanding what others have without making efforts to get the same for oneself.

17. Attempting to get what others have by stealth or aggression.

18. Being in constant difficulties with the law.

19. Indulgence in behavior that injures one's body or mind or impedes their functioning.

20. Needless self-torment over past events or presumed failures.

21. Engaging in extremely hazardous or exceptionally difficult activities for the purpose of proving oneself to be worthwhile or to overcome other's criticism or ridicule.

22. Fear of, or dislike for, engaging in activities largely because they are considered vital or desirable by the large majority of people in one's own culture.

23. Chronic or intermittent states of depression or anxiety.

24. Unreasonable fears.

25. Excessive angers.

26. Persistent behavior that arouses hostility or avoidance on the part of other people.

27. Excessive enthusiasm.[21]

Rational Self-Analysis

The purpose of a Rational Self-Analysis (RSA) is to force one to think rationally and quickly rid himself of negative and irrational emotions. "It is a rational analysis of how you direct your brain," says Maultsby.[22] The RSA format (see Appendix B, page 147) is ideally adapted to helping people get a more realistic view of the situations to which they have responded emotionally. The self-talk section is very successful in uncovering the thinking of which people are not usually aware. The section on rational alternatives lends itself to the pastor-counselor as a wonderful opportunity to present Scriptural solutions.

The format of an RSA is to be so well learned by the counselee that he can do an RSA in his own mind when he is not able to sit down with pen and paper. When facing an emotionally upsetting situation, it should become normal to resort to the RSA technique. Many proponents of Rational Behavior Therapy recommend that the RSA format be taught to high school students to help prepare them to face the difficulties of life that are certain to come.

As-if RSAs

As-if RSAs are to give one practice in doing RSAs by using someone else's problems. Here are a few reasons for using someone else's problems:

1. The student may not have a problem at present.

2. Doing several different RSAs will give him an opportunity to gain understanding, skill and confidence. It is the safest way to learn this method before he works on his own problems.

3. The student can learn much about himself. People reared in the same society tend to have the same rational and irrational beliefs. When we see something irrational in others, we often recognize the same irrationality in ourselves. We do not usually see ourselves as others see us, but we can learn about ourselves by looking at others. Maultsby and others believe "the most impressive things to you about other people usually are the positive or

negative traits that you have, have had, or wish to have."[23] While reading the problems of others, the student can expect to obtain many views of his own personality. The student is to read the *A, B, C* and *E* sections of the real person's problem and to imagine that he is that person. He is to try to solve the problem using the camera check for the *A* section and using the rules for rational thinking to challenge the self-talk of the *B* section. His aim is to see if he can find rational alternatives to the self-talk which will enable him to replace the old emotion at *C* with the new one at *E*. Next, the student checks his evaluation of the *A, B* and *C* sections against that of both the real person and the therapist. Maultsby's book *Help Yourself to Happiness* contains some examples of As-if RSAs.[24]

Rational Emotive Imagery (REI)

Rational Self-Analysis not only helps us to analyze our problems but also helps solve the problems by encouraging us to become more rational in our self-talk. In addition to altering one's thinking, emoting and acting by means of RSAs, rational self-counseling offers us Rational Emotive Imagery to help us overcome the persistence of our old irrational thoughts. Long-standing emotional habits do not just roll over and die merely because we do not want them anymore.

The persistence of our thinking, emotions and actions is the result of the learning process itself. We form habits. The seemingly automatic responses we make to certain stimuli are the result of habit. Something happens, and we respond almost instantaneously, without even thinking. This "something" is a cue, like the sound of the bell in the Pavlov experiment in which the dog responds to something that has become associated with an original stimulus. When people experience a cue, they usually are unaware of it and wonder what made them react as they did.

Goodman relates a story that Maultsby used to illustrate cues. It concerns a man who had "a history of getting depressed at 5 P.M. because he knew that he would find something to quarrel with his wife about before the evening was over and he would end up miserable."[25] The man knew that he often quarreled when he went home, but he was not so aware of the depressed feeling he experienced when it was time to go home. **The cuing effect is the reason for much failure in counseling.** The person knows what needs to be changed and he wants to change it, but he finds himself failing to do what he would like to do in his spontaneous responses. Being unaware of the cues creates the illusion of "being compelled" to respond to a stimulus in a particular way.

An RSA is usually effective in bringing out the habitual self-talk that serves as the cue. It can also help us to substitute more rational thinking for the cue. But there is still further need of help in changing the way a person responds to a particular stimulus. An REI can give him that help.

Deep breathing relaxation technique. Before doing an REI, Maultsby recommends helping the counselee to a relatively anxiety-free state so that he will begin to pair a calm feeling with the problem situation instead of his usual fear. He suggests deep breathing exercises for this purpose. Deep breathing exercises may be very helpful to the counselee who shows much tension. Anxiety is often suppressed by tensing the body—holding the breath and pulling in the stomach, resulting in the chest being held high in the breathing-in position. This hinders the deep breathing that is necessary for proper metabolism. The final result is a loss of energy (tiredness) and a lowering of emotional tone. Gross quotes Lowen as saying, "The reason so many people breathe badly is that they are afraid to feel emotion . . . The truly healthy person breathes with his whole body."[26] Teaching people to breathe deeply will help them at least temporarily to be in touch with their emotions.

Lowen uses a unique method for deep breathing. His client stands in front of a two foot high stool that has a rolled up blanket upon it. The client then arches himself backward over the stool while keeping his mouth open. As the body adapts to the stress, the breathing becomes deeper.[27]

Maultsby's method of deep breathing is described here:

1. In one slow but continuous motion, take in a deep breath and force it all out. As you are breathing out, think just one word: "Relax."

2. At the end of breathing out, hold your breath for at least ten seconds. To estimate the seconds count: "one thousand one, one thousand two . . . etc." It takes about a second to say "one thousand one."

3. Keep repeating the above steps for two or three minutes or as long as it takes for you to feel calm.[28]

When in a calm frame of mind the counselee pictures in his mind the corrected *A* section (*Da*) and *sees* himself thinking or saying only the rational thoughts of his *Db* section, and makes himself feel only the feelings he described in his *E* section (see appendix, page 147).

Practicing the feeling state for an action you are learning is called *emotive imagery*. It enables a person to overcome what is known as *cognitive dissonance*—feeling wrong when you are doing right.

Rational Emotive Imagery is like playing a game with yourself. You are mentally putting yourself in a situation and then getting the right feeling about it. You imagine yourself thinking rationally and when the situation arises the next time, you might not be so quick to do the wrong thing. You are reeducating your thinking and emotions in a practice situation rather than in a real life situation.

<u>A sample REI.</u> Maultsby gives us a sample REI script:

I am in my boss's office. He's sitting behind his desk holding a letter. He says, "This letter you just typed has a dozen typing errors in it. Don't ever give me trash like that again, or it will be the last time you do."

I think, "He's a fallible human being as I am. He should say what he is saying because this is what his past experience and his present thinking are leading him to say. I can't control what he thinks or says, but by being calm and rational right now, I'll be more likely to influence him to become calm. He has a right to say whatever he chooses to. What he says doesn't make me a bad

person. I am a fallible human being and my mistakes only prove I am fallible. If I can make a mistake, it's good to know about it so I can learn from it."
Therefore, I calm myself with the instant Better Feeling Maneuver and then calmly go over to the desk and get the letter and say, "I'm sorry. I wasn't aware of the mistakes. I will retype the letter. Next time I will be sure to proofread it much more carefully."[29]

Rational Emotive Imagery is also very effective in conquering phobias, the debilitating and irrational fears that are experienced by approximately one in ten of us. If counselees could endure repeatedly, in their imaginations, feared situations for about fifteen to twenty seconds, while in a relaxed state, and tell themselves rational thoughts about the situation, the panic connected with the phobia would soon subside.

The reason some phobics fail to overcome their fears is because they are afraid or refuse to confront them. An effective way to confront them is by means of Rational Emotive Imagery.

<u>Autoaversive imagery.</u> Another form of emotive imagery is called autoaversive imagery. It is helpful in seeking to eliminate some very well-learned or compulsive behavior. Excessive drinking, smoking or eating are habits that often yield to this type of imagery. The object is to practice pairing something very repulsive with the thing desired. Maultsby suggests that the compulsive eater imagine vomit on top of the food that is his greatest temptation. A drunkard could picture himself in a bloody automobile accident. A smoker might place himself in the cancer ward of a hospital. When the repulsive image and its accompanying emotions are habitually paired with the thing desired, behavior is likely to be changed so as to avoid the immediate negative consequences.

Summarizing the process of liberation from irrational thinking

The process of getting rid of our irrational thoughts takes place in several steps:

1. Making the valid insight that a thought is irrational.

2. Making a sincere announcement of forsaking the irrational thought.

3. Refusing to use the irrational thought to explain present life experience.

4. Explaining the old and present life experiences in the light of the new rational thought.

5. Acting in accordance with rational thinking, even though feeling wrong about it (cognitive dissonance).

6. Imagining yourself acting in accordance with the new rational thought that you are convinced is best for you to adopt.

7. Practicing the new behavior that integrates your perceptions, thoughts and feelings. The new behavior is now normal and natural because actions, perceptions, thoughts and feelings are all logical for each other and support each other. It feels right.

Summary

Rational Behavior Therapy in its modified form as set forth in this book is very highly recommended as a counseling method for born-again pastors who make the Bible their ultimate authority. It is recommended for the following reasons:

1. No Biblical doctrine is compromised.

2. No valid psychological presupposition is contradicted.

3. It does not depend upon nebulous psychological jargon.

4. It does not require extensive training in psychology.

5. It is not a lengthy, time-consuming method of counseling.

6. It teaches a person to be his own counselor.

7. It is very practical in helping *normal* people to solve their problems.

8. It does not hinder, but rather aids, in reaching the goals set forth in chapter 6.

9. While it does not employ all of the uncovering techniques set forth in chapter 7, it certainly does not preclude the use of any of them by the counselor.

10. Every one of the therapeutic approaches of chapter 8 can be easily incorporated by the counselor into the RSA format

when talking about rational alternatives.

11. It recommends a warm, loving and accepting approach.

12. It is highly directive in its approach, like the Scriptures.

13. It faces up to the human tendency to distort the truth.

14. It emphasizes facing reality.

15. It emphasizes taking responsibility for one's own emotions and actions.

16. It does not involve a prolonged and deep probing of the unconscious past but deals primarily with the past or unconscious that is influencing one's present thinking.

17. It provides an easily understandable and psychologically acceptable view of emotions.

18. It emphasizes the place of the will in bringing about a change in oneself (the Christian recognizes the limitations of man's power of choice).

19. Its view of the importance of thinking coincides exactly with that of the Scriptures (Prov. 23:7).

20. It recognizes the importance of understanding how one thinks about himself (self-esteem).

21. It can offer a counselee hope in the first session.

It is my earnest prayer that this overview of the major issues of counseling will encourage many to become more deeply involved in the ministry of counseling. If pastors would seek a better understanding of the minds of those to whom they minister and of God's great and effective resources for meeting spiritual and emotional needs, they could be more effectively used of the Lord to bring relief and peace to troubled hearts.

Appendix A
Explanation and Procedure of a Rational Self-Analysis

The procedure is set forth in the following steps, which must be taken consecutively:

1. Ask, What is your problem?
Have the person write down under *A* all the facts concerning this problem. (See Appendix B for a sample of the worksheet.) Have him describe the actual event leading to the unpleasant emotion.

2. Ask, How do (did) you feel about it?
Under *C*, the person is to describe how he felt—sad, angry, depressed, nervous, fearful, etc. Ask him to rate the degree of the emotion (example: sad, 50%; angry, 75%).

3. Ask, How would you like to feel about it?
Under *E* the person is to write down how he would like to feel about the problem—calm, optimistic, etc.

4. Ask, What did you do?
Be sure to include this under *A*.

5. Ask, How would you have liked to have acted?
This does not need to be recorded (emotional goals are recorded under *E*).

6. Say, Let's do a camera check of *A*.
Have the person write under *Da* only what a tape recorder or a camera could pick up. Exclude feelings, opinions and attitudes.

7. Ask the person to write out all the self-talk (numbering each sentence), the spontaneous evaluations, beliefs, attitudes and opinions under *B*.

8. Ask, Is each statement based on the rules of rationality?
Have the counselee check each sentence under *B* with the rules of rational thinking. If the thinking is not in accord with rules 1, 6 or 7, it is not rational. And if it is not in accord with a total of five out of the seven rules, it is not rational. Ask, Is the statement rational, then?

9. For every sentence of self-talk under *B* that is not judged rational, have the person write under *Db* a personally acceptable alternative.

10. Suggest or admonish concerning alternative ways of thinking (use ideas from chapter 8 on therapeutic approaches).

11. Ask, What have you learned from this session?

12. Ask, What will you do about this insight? (Do not accept "I will *try to*" but only "I *will do*.")

13. Ask, Would it not be profitable for you to do an RSA on ________? (homework assignment).

Rules for Rational Thinking:
1. It is based on objective reality.
2. It protects your life.
3. It helps you achieve your goals.
4. It keeps you out of trouble with others.
5. It eliminates significant emotional conflict.
6. It is based upon spiritual realities.
7. It is based upon Scriptural principles.

Appendix B
Format of a Rational Self-Analysis

A
Facts and Events
(Describe the actual events lead-
ing to the unpleasant emotion.)

Da
Camera Check of *A*

B

Db
**Rational Debate of *B* (if self-talk
is irrational). Personally Acceptable Alternatives:**

B1

Db1

B2

Db2

B3

Db3

B4

Db4

C	*E*
Emotional Consequences of *B* (Observe the degree of the emotion. Example: sad, 50%.)	Emotional Goals for Future (How you would like to feel.)

Appendix C
A Sample RSA (done by a man we will call "Joe")

A

Facts and Events

My wife and I attended a dinner party which included six other couples, most of whom I did not know. As I began to partake of the hors d'oeuvres, I realized that I didn't want to be there. I felt isolated and I couldn't involve myself with the others.

B

Self-talk

1. I don't enjoy mingling with others; I don't feel at ease.
2. I am unable to involve myself with others.

Da

Camera Check of *A*

Not wanting to be there may not have been picked up by the camera, nor could my feeling of being isolated. The camera could have picked up an appearance of boredom. The tape recorder may confirm that I did not have as much to say as the others did.

Db

Rational Challenge of *B*
And possible alternatives

1. Can't be challenged.

2. Not rational because:
   a. The camera or tape recorder cannot confirm it.
   b. Such thinking has no relationship to life-preservation.
   c. Such thinking does not help me to achieve my goals.
   d. Such thinking could cause conflict with others.

Db continued

    e. Such thinking causes conflict within myself.

    f. Such thinking does not have anything to do with spiritual reality.

    g. Such thinking is contrary to the counsel of Proverbs 18:24, "A man that hath friends must show himself friendly."

(Usually *Db* is on the right hand side of the paper, but to conserve space in this illustration, it will be written on the whole page.)

COUNSELOR: Then according to RBT's rules for rational thinking, is your thinking rational or not?

    (Joe agreed that his thinking was irrational.)

COUNSELOR: Would you take this thought and give it a rational alternative?

JOE: I am not unable to relate to others, because sometimes I do involve myself with others.

COUNSELOR: You have a good intellect, and good appearance.

JOE: In some situations I *choose* not to do it, but I am *able* to relate to others.

COUNSELOR: How could you look at others?

JOE: Some folks would be friendly, if I chose to give them a chance—but not all of them.

COUNSELOR: I think that you are seeing that some of these people, whom you have been thinking of as unfriendly, could become warm friends if you gave them half a chance.

JOE: Yes, that's true. Previously, I saw my problem as a reaction to what I saw in them—but now I see that the problem is with me.

COUNSELOR: Remember Proverbs 18:24, "A man that hath friends must show himself friendly."

JOE: But sometimes these people will behave in some way that will cause me to feel very critical of them.

COUNSELOR: You probably need to ask yourself if it is happening with too many people. This sort of thing does happen to all of us, but if it happens in too many of your relationships, maybe the problem is not with them, but with your own thinking.

JOE: Yes, I am willing to admit it is always my thinking—

Db continued

	I shouldn't be so inflexible, it seems to me. It would be better if I were flexible and more capable of responding to others.
COUNSELOR:	Could it be that you are expecting perfection or too much of others—before you feel that you want their friendship?
JOE:	I am almost thinking the opposite. I wonder if I am not expecting perfection of myself and I'm afraid they won't find it when they actually get to know me.
COUNSELOR:	Can you see what you have done? You have turned things right around. You began by saying you saw so many flaws in others that you didn't want their friendship. Now you are saying that you are afraid others will see so many flaws in you that they will not like you. *(Note: He has been practicing the defense mechanisms of projection and psychic withdrawal.)* What is the solution to that?
JOE:	I realize that *nobody* is perfect and that I certainly am not. I am a fallible human being.
COUNSELOR:	Do you think it would help you to realize that others have perhaps as many faults as you have?
JOE:	Yes, I certainly should be the first one to realize that.

B continued	*Db* continued
3. I don't want to be here but I don't have a good reason for feeling this way.	3. Joe is admitting that there is no rationality to his not wanting to be there.
4. It's a burden.	4. The rules of rationality show such thinking is not rational.
5. I'm not certain I like all the people present.	5. The rules of rationality show such thinking is not rational.
6. I don't see friendliness in others very often.	6. The rules of rationality show such thinking is not rational.
7. People seem tied up in their own interests and ideas and seem defensive about them.	7. (Using the rules of rationality, Joe agreed that this thinking was not rational.)

COUNSELOR: Is there some alternative way of thinking?

Db continued

JOE: People will act the way they choose, but I don't have to allow that to arouse negative reactions in me, unless I choose to allow it.

COUNSELOR: You still haven't changed your mind about *them*. You still think of *them* as being self-centered. The only thing you have realized is that you don't have to react to others the way you have been.

JOE: That's right!

COUNSELOR: Is there not another possibility?

JOE: That *they* are not self-centered! Perhaps I am the self-centered one. I want them to pay too much attention to me.

COUNSELOR: Could it not be that your self-centeredness causes you to think that *they* are only interested in themselves? *(Projection is showing up again.)*

JOE: Yes, sometimes I see what I want to see in others so that I can justify leaving early; then I don't have to walk around feeling foolish. *(Rationalization is going on here.)*

COUNSELOR: You are actually saying that they are not friendly, when you are hiding the fact that you are ill at ease and want to get out of there—which is the real reason you say "They

Db continued

are unfriendly." *(He was practicing a form of denial here.)*

JOE: Yeah, that's very interesting.

8. (Joe agreed that his thinking was irrational.)

COUNSELOR: What is the main reason you see your thinking as irrational?

JOE: Because some of them did find satisfaction in relating to others.

COUNSELOR: What rational alternative could you give to this kind of thinking?

JOE: If it is important to me, I could latch onto a floater and take the initiative in relating to him.

COUNSELOR: What would you think would be one of the most important factors *in yourself* which would cause you to become a good friend of somebody?

JOE: I think I would have to be interested in them as persons.

COUNSELOR: Concerned?

JOE: Oh, yes.

COUNSELOR: If you feel a concern for another person you probably can make that person your friend.

JOE: I've said that to hundreds of people. Why can't I incorporate this into my own life?

COUNSELOR: Could I ask, do you have a real interest in

B continued

8. I seem to see a bunch of isolated figures floating around the room, sometimes talking to one another—not relating in ways that are meaningful.

> *Db* continued
>
> those who seem unfriendly to you?
>
> JOE: Clearly, not all the time.
>
> COUNSELOR: Maybe your thoughts are upon yourself. You are wondering whether or not you are going to be accepted?
>
> JOE: Why are they not concerned with me? Why don't they show me some . . . ?
>
> COUNSELOR: We have already agreed how this kind of thinking is self-defeating. Do you think you could think of other people as being needy people?

COUNSELOR: As a minister, I am convinced that every person is a needy person—even the hardest, the most callous, those who have placed barriers about themselves. Deep down they all have needs. That person which you might think is selfish, isolated and cold—have you ever stopped to think that he is a needy person?

JOE: Certainly not at those times!

COUNSELOR: Would it help you to practice thinking about others as being needy people who need friendship?

JOE: Definitely, it would.

COUNSELOR: If when you go to your next social, would it not make a difference if you told yourself, "There are some other lonely people out there and I'm not going to be concerned about how friendly they are to me, but I'm going to be concerned about them and make them feel that I am glad that they are there." Would that make a difference?

NOTE: The counselee agreed that it would—but then expressed another psychological insight that was dawning on him. He was afraid that a relationship might become too close and that the relationship might demand too much of him.

COUNSELOR: Are you afraid of the demands which will be made upon you?

Db continued

JOE: Right! (Nervous laughter followed.) Their needs might really come out—they might really need to talk—that person might really be sick and not have anything interesting to say. And I may have to spend my time there—and shoot my evening.

(The element of selfishness is showing up. If dealing with Christians, Rationality Rule #7 applies.)

COUNSELOR: And there could be other demands upon friendship. Don't you have to weigh the cost of being a friend against the cost of not being a friend? Here you find yourself isolated, depressed and sad—that's the price you are paying for not being a friend. Which has the greater cost—being a friend or not being one? And friendships are so rewarding—I'm sure that mentally you are aware of this.

NOTE: Joe made the observation that so much of his day at work as a professional psychologist involved the giving of himself to those who needed him. And to have to do that again in a social situation seemed almost too much of a burden. "I want others to want me and need me without costing me anything. That is obviously irrational and you can't do it," he said. He stated that he found satisfaction and a good feeling in meeting the needs of others while at work during the day.

COUNSELOR: What makes you think that you wouldn't feel the same way in a social setting?

JOE: I have experiences which I have *chosen* to see as negative. I have not maintained the same attitude that I have when I am working at my profession!

NOTE: Joe stated that often he found himself trying to get what *he wanted* from a conversation—intellectual stimulation—and then turning people off because of challenging them too much or threatening them somewhat because he is a psychologist.

COUNSELOR: Do you consider yourself a loner?

JOE: Yes, I believe you have put your finger on a very significant fact.

COUNSELOR: You realize that such thinking is not rational?

JOE: Yes, I realize today that the problem is not with others but with my thinking.

Db continued

COUNSELOR:	Could you do something in the way of imagery which would help you?
JOE:	I'm not certain that I understand you.
COUNSELOR:	Could you practice imagining something four times a day for ten minutes that could help you overcome your "loner" thinking?
JOE:	Do you mean imagining myself going up to a stranger in a social situation and taking the initiative to draw that person into a discussion—holding out my hand and saying, "I am Joe . . ."? The interesting thing is that when I have done that I have been eminently successful.
COUNSELOR:	There's your key. Why not keep on repeating that success—even though you don't feel like it. By doing it over and over, pretty soon you will *feel* differently about what you are doing and it will become a habit.

B continued	*Db* continued
9. I feel as though I am intruding.	9. COUNSELOR: You have decided that such thinking is irrational. What is an alternative way of thinking about this? JOE: I have not been rejected all that much. My perceptions have been overly influenced by the past, which has no relevance now. NOTE: I pointed out to Joe that it would be very unusual in such a social setting for someone to think one is intruding when trying to initiate a conversation.
10. I feel I could be rebuffed or rejected.	10. Joe agreed that this thinking was irrational. I pointed out that *fear* should also be placed under *E* (Emotional Response), and noted the possibility of low self-

Db continued

esteem being a factor in his problem.

Joe agreed and said he really wanted genuine love and acceptance—to feel appreciated and respected.

B continued

(added during the counseling session.)

11. Maybe I am not capable of meeting whatever may be their standards for meaningful relationships.

C

Emotional Consequences of *B*
Felt isolated and ill at ease, sad, depressed, unhappy.
Feel inadequate to solve my problem (despair).

E

Emotional Goals for Future
How would you like to feel?

Comfortable, at ease and happy and cheerful at social events.

(Added during counseling session.)

Fear of not being capable of meeting their standards for a meaningful relationship.

(Added during counseling session.)

To feel genuine love and acceptance.
To feel respected and appreciated.

An examination of the previous conversation between a counselor and a counselee as they go over a Rational Self-Analysis reveals many things:

1. It serves as an uncovering technique—bringing out material not originally included in the RSA.

2. It reveals to the counselor various defense mechanisms which can help him in diagnosing and in giving counsel.

3. It provides opportunity for the counselee to gain insight.

4. It gives a natural opportunity for the counselor to confront, admonish, probe and suggest solutions.

Notes

Chapter 1

1. Gary Collins, *How to be a People Helper* (Santa Ana, CA: Vision House, 1976), 31.

2. Theodore Roszak, "Getting Your Head Together," *Newsweek* (September 6, 1976): 57.

3. James Sire, *The Universe Next Door: A Basic World View Catalog* (Downers Grove, IL: InterVarsity Press, 1976), 161.

4. Marvin Stone, "Our Solipsist Society," *U.S. News & World Report* (September 5, 1978): 100.

5. Ibid.

6. Martin L. Gross, *The Psychological Society* (New York: Random House, 1978), 4.

7. O. Hobert Mowrer, cited by Jay E. Adams, *Competent to Counsel* (Grand Rapids: Baker Book House, 1970), xvi.

Chapter 2

1. Harold J. Haas, *Pastoral Counseling* (St. Louis: Concordia Pub. House, 1970), 59.

2. Ibid.

3. Ibid., 60.

4. Ibid., 38.

5. Collins, *How to be a People Helper,* 13.

6. Paul A. Hauck, *Reason in Pastoral Counseling* (Philadelphia: The Westminster Press, 1982), 17.

7. Meyer Friedman and Ray H. Rosenman, *Type A Behavior and Your Heart* (New York: Alfred A. Knopf, 1974), 166.

8. Ibid., 167.

9. Ibid.

10. Ibid., 168.

11. Ibid., 169.

12. James Dobson, *Hide or Seek* (Old Tappan, NJ: Fleming H. Revell Co., 1974), 11.

13. Gross, *The Psychological Society,* 250.

14. Ibid., 251.

15. Adams, *Competent to Counsel,* 41.

16. Albert Ellis and Robert A. Harper, *A New Guide to Rational Living* (Englewood Cliffs, NJ: Prentice-Hall, 1975), 220.

17. Gross, 227.

18. Monte H. Liebman, *Introduction to Psychotherapy* (Brookfield, WI: Med-Psych Pub., 1977), 2.

Chapter 3

1. Howard J. Clinebell, Jr., *Basic Types of Pastoral Counseling* (Nashville: Abingdon Press, 1966), 298.

2. Dean Johnson, cited by Clinebell, 294.

3. Clinebell, 297.

4. Haas, *Pastoral Counseling,* 180, 181.

5. Basil Jackson, "Psychology, Psychiatry and the Pastor," *Bibliotheca Sacra,* vol. 2 (1975): 102.

6. Alphonse Calabrese and William Proctor, *Rx: The Christian Love-Treatment* (Garden City, NY: Doubleday & Co., 1976), 32.

7. Ibid., 33.

8. Nathaniel Branden, *The Disowned Self* (Los Angeles: Nash Pub. Corp., 1971), 93.

9. Robert A. Harper, *Psychoanalysis and Psychotherapy, 36 Systems* (Englewood Cliffs, NJ: Prentice-Hall, 1959), 92.

10. Collins, *How to be a People Helper,* 33.

11. Haas, 171.

12. Jackson, 103.

13. Ibid., 104.

14. Clinebell, 296.

15. Joseph Wolpe, cited by Harper, 110.

16. Charles R. Solomon, *Counseling With the Mind of Christ. The Dynamics of Spirituotherapy* (Old Tappan, NJ: F. H. Revell, 1977), 18.

Chapter 4

1. William Glasser, *Reality Therapy, a New Approach to Psychiatry* (New York: Harper & Row, 1975), 69.

2. Ellis, *Rational Living,* 114.

3. John W. Drakeford, *Integrity Therapy* (Nashville: Broadman Press, 1961), 17.

4. Ibid., 18.

5. Albert C. Outler, *Psychotherapy and the Christian Message* (New York: Harper and Row, 1954), 86.

6. J.D. Radcliff, "I Am Joe's Brain," *Reader's Digest* (April 1974): 91.

7. Jess Lair, *I Ain't Much, Baby - But I'm All I've Got* (Garden City, NY: Doubleday & Co., 1969), 15.

8. Adams, *Competent to Counsel,* 61.

9. Joel Kovel, *A Complete Guide to Therapy from Psychoanalysis to Behavior Modification* (New York: Pantheon Books, 1976), 41.

10. Liebman, *Introduction to Psychotherapy,* 1.

11. Alphonse Maeder, cited by Raymond L. Cramer, *The Psychology of Jesus & Mental Health* (Grand Rapids: Zondervan, 1959), 14.

12. David E. Roberts, *Psychotherapy and a Christian View of Man* (New York: Charles Scribner's Sons, 1950), 134.

13. Maxie Maultsby, Jr., *Help Yourself to Happiness* (New York: Institute for Rational Living, 1975), 11.

14. Basil Jackson, psychiatrist, in a lecture at California Graduate School of Theology, Milwaukee extension, November 8, 1978. Permission to quote secured.

15. Gross, *The Psychological Society,* 10.

16. Jackson, "Psychology, Psychiatry and the Pastor," 11.

17. Ibid., 12.

18. Branden, *The Disowned Self,* xi.

19. Roberts, 94.

20. Ibid., 99.

21. Clinebell, *Basic Types of Pastoral Counseling,* 31.

22. Paul Tournier, *The Best of Paul Tournier* (New York: Iverson-Norman Associates, 1977), 64, 67, 70.

23. Drakeford, 32–34.

Chapter 5

1. J.P. Chaplin, *Dictionary of Psychology* (New York: Dell Publishing Co., 1968), 415.

2. Branden, *The Disowned Self,* 41, 42.

3. Otto Fenichel, *The Psychoanalytic Theory of Neurosis* (New York: W.W. Norton & Co., 1945), 15.

4. Nathaniel Branden, *The Psychology of Self-Esteem* (Los Angeles: Nash Publishing Corporation, 1969), 20.

5. Branden, *The Disowned Self,* 47.

6. Robert W. White, *The Abnormal Personality* (New York: The Ronald Press, 1956), 195.

7. White, 42.

8. Roberts, *Psychotherapy,* 110.

9. Gross, *The Psychological Society,* 321, 322.

10. Chaplin, 33.

11. Gross, 324.

12. Harper quoting Otto Rank, *Psychoanalysis,* 53.

13. Cramer, *Psychology of Jesus,* 34.

14. Jackson, "Psychology, Psychiatry and the Pastor," 108.

15. Raymond J. McCall, *The Varieties of Abnormality* (Springfield, IL: Charles C. Thomas, 1975), 37.

16. Milton Layden, *Escaping the Hostility Trap* (Englewood Cliffs, NJ: Prentice-Hall, 1977), 10.

17. Cramer, 39.

18. Harper, 23.

19. White, 229.

20. Basil Jackson, "Repression," a class hand-out paper, California Graduate School of Theology, Milwaukee extension, 1978.

21. Gross, 189.

22. White, 275.

23. Ibid., 233.

24. Cramer, 47.

25. Basil Jackson, in a class lecture, California Graduate School of Theology, Milwaukee extension, 1978.

26. Fenichel, 19.

27. White, 266.

28. Basil Jackson, "Categories of Mental Symptoms," in a class hand-out paper, California Graduate School of Theology, Milwaukee extension, 1978.

29. McCall, 65.

30. Ibid., 70.

31. White, 525.

32. Ibid., 279.

33. McCall, 115, 116.

34. Ibid., 74.

35. Norman L. Mitchell, quoting Dr. Vernon Riley, *Ministry.* Journal published by the General Conference of Seventh-Day Adventists, Hagerstown, MD. (1982): 26.

36. McCall, 255.

37. Clinebell, *Pastoral Counseling,* 36.

38. Glasser, *Reality Therapy,* 37.

39. Ibid., 62.

40. Adams, *Competent to Counsel,* 151.

41. Ibid., 151, 152.

42. O. Quentin Hyder, *The Christian's Handbook of Psychiatry* (Old Tappan, NJ: Fleming H. Revell Co., 1971), 155.

43. Basil Jackson, a statement in a personal interview, Milwaukee, December, 1978.

44. Jackson, "Psychology, Psychiatry and the Pastor," 10.

45. Ibid.

46. Roberts, 111.

47. Ibid., 48.

48. Clinebell, 31.

49. Ellis, *Rational Living*, 21.

50. Branden, *The Disowned Self*, 6.

51. Ibid., 69.

52. Ibid., 71.

53. Ibid., 44.

54. Ibid., 71.

55. Ellis, 98.

56. William H. Fitts, *The Experience of Psychotherapy* (Princeton, NJ: D. Van Nostrand Co., 1965), 9.

57. Jackson, "Psychology, Psychiatry and the Pastor," 8.

58. Outler, *Psychotherapy*, 73.

59. Glasser, 162, 165.

60. Ibid., 33–35.

61. Ibid., 162.

62. Ibid., 32.

63. Clinebell, 33.

64. Sire, *The Universe Next Door*, 103, 104.

65. Joseph Hart, "Feeling Therapy," an abstract published by The Center For Feeling, 1017 South LaBrea Ave., Los Angeles, 1978, 1.

66. Ibid.

67. Bruce Maliver, cited by Martin Gross, 301, 302.

68. Ellis, 137.

69. Haas, *Pastoral Counseling*, 45.

70. Branden, *The Disowned Self*, 27.

71. Ibid., xi.

72. Drakeford, *Integrity Therapy*, 10.

73. Ibid., 54.

74. Ellis, 6.

75. Sidney M. Jourard, *The Transparent Self* (New York: Van Nostrand Reinhold Co., 1971), 32.

76. Ibid., 27–33.

77. Ibid., 33.

78. Drakeford, 89.

79. Lair, *I Ain't Much, Baby,* 44.

Chapter 6

1. Harper, *Psychoanalysis,* 154.
2. Branden, *The Disowned Self,* 10.
3. Ibid., 82, 83.
4. Ibid., 4.
5. Roberts, *Christian View of Man,* 97.
6. Harper, 65.
7. Ibid., 66.
8. Liebman, *Introduction to Psychotherapy,* 8, 9.
9. Ibid., 2.
10. Drakeford, *Integrity Therapy,* 27.
11. Harper, 125.

Chapter 7

1. Basil Jackson, statement in class notes, California Graduate School of Theology, Milwaukee extension, December, 1978.
2. Margaret O. Hyde and Edward S. Marks, *Psychology in Action,* 2d ed. (New York: NcGraw-Hill Book Co., 1976), 22.
3. Paul D. Morris, *Love Therapy* (Wheaton, IL: Tyndale House Publishers, 1974), 46.
4. White, *The Abnormal Personality,* 267.
5. Branden, *The Disowned Self,* 32.
6. The Johari Window, a model developed by Joseph Luft and Harry Ingham cited in a seminar by Dr. Nancy Duvall, business & professional seminar, Rosemead, CA, 1976.
7. Gross, *The Psychological Society,* 188.
8. Edward Cole, statement in class, California Graduate School of Theology, Milwaukee extension, October, 1978.
9. Branden, 90.
10. Chaplin, *Dictionary of Psychology,* 196.
11. White, 187.
12. Harper, *Psychoanalysis,* 19.
13. White, 330.
14. Branden, 17.
15. Ibid., 17, 97.
16. Ibid., 17.
17. Ibid., 10.
18. Calabrese, *RX: The Christian Love-Treatment,* 49, 50.

Chapter 8

1. Rollo May, *The Courage To Create* (New York: W.W. Norton & Co., 1975), 79–81.
2. Harper, *Psychoanalysis,* 153.
3. Martyn Lloyd-Jones, cited by O. Quentin Hyder, *The Christian's Handbook,* 40, 41.
4. Calabrese, *RX: The Christian Love-Treatment,* 61.
5. Craig W. Ellison, ed., *Self-Esteem* (Oklahoma City: Southwestern Press, for Christian Association of Psychological Studies, 1976), 3.
6. Dr. O. Hobart Mowrer of the University of Illinois, in an address at the Wednesday night convocation of Religion-in-Life Week at Iowa State University, January 20, 1960.
7. Jackson, "Psychology, Psychiatry and the Pastor," 15.
8. Ibid., 1:12–14.
9. Viktor E. Frankl, *Man's Search for Meaning* (New York: Washington Square Press, 1963), 154.
10. Branden, *The Disowned Self,* 69.
11. Colin Wilson, *New Pathways in Psychology: Maslow and the Post-Freudian Revolution* (London: Victor Gollancz, 1972), 68.
12. Branden, 69.

Chapter 9

1. Katinka Matson, *The Psychology Today Omnibook of Personal Development* (New York: William Morrow and Co., 1977), 160.
2. Goodman, *Well Being,* 196.
3. Ibid. 198.
4. Ibid., 201.
5. Ellis, *Rational Living,* 12.
6. Ibid., 14.
7. Gross, *The Psychological Society,* 316.
8. Ellis, 25.
9. Ibid., 21.
10. Maxie C. Maultsby, Jr., *Handbook of Rational Self-Counseling* (Lexington: University of Kentucky Medical Center, 1971), 41, 42.
11. Branden, *The Psychology of Self-Esteem,* 223.
12. Ibid., 224.
13. Goodman, 38.
14. Ellis, 16.
15. Ibid., 21.
16. Maxie Maultsby, Jr., *Help Yourself to Happiness* (New York: Institute

for Rational Living, Inc., 1975), 29.

17. Ibid., 23.

18. Ibid., 56.

19. Basil Jackson, statement in class notes, California Graduate School of Theology, Milwaukee extension, October, 1977.

20. Goodman, 39, 40.

21. Ibid., 40, 41.

22. Maultsby, *Help Yourself,* 55.

23. Ibid, 105.

24. Ibid., 107–130.

25. Goodman, 61.

26. Gross, 292.

27. Ibid.

28. Maultsby, *Help Yourself,* 90.

29. Maxie Maultsby, Jr., REI Script Format, Lexington: University of Kentucky College of Medicine, 1976.

Glossary

ABREACTION. The discharge of tension by reliving in words, feelings and actions a traumatic experience.

ANXIETY DISORDERS. Anxiety attacks in which one's fears grow altogether beyond one's control. Usually the person does not know precisely what he is afraid of, but his body reacts just as it would to an outward physical threat.

AUTISTIC. Tending to be withdrawn and extremely preoccupied with one's own thoughts and fantasies (sometimes lost in a world of inner fantasy).

AUTOAVERSIVE IMAGERY. The practice of pairing in our minds something very repulsive with the thing we desire—yet really want to rid ourselves of for our good.

AUTONOMY. The state of self-regulation.

CAMERA CHECK. A procedure used in doing a Rational Self-Analysis in which the counselee looks at the problem or situation just as a camera would. Its purpose is to remove all subjective elements from the "picture."

CATATONIC. A disorder in which patients appear to be in a stupor, showing extreme negativism and inaccessibility to outside stimuli.

CATHARSIS. The release of tensions and anxieties by reliving and unburdening those traumatic incidents which, in the past, were originally associated with the repression of the emotions.

COGNITIVE DISSONANCE. Feeling wrong about something one is doing when he knows it is right.

COGNITIVE-EMOTIVE-BEHAVIORISTIC. An approach in psychology that teaches that by disciplining one's *thinking,* he will be enabled to live an emotionally satisfying and self-fulfilling life.

COMPENSATION. The process of engaging in substitute behavior in order to make up for social or physical frustration or lack of ability in a certain area of personality.

CONDITIONING MODEL. Shaping one's behavior by repeated exposure to particular conditions, with which responses become associated.

CONVERSION. The transformation of a psychological conflict into physical symptoms.

COPING. Realistically acknowledging a deficiency and attempting on a conscious level to modify the defect.

COUNTERACTION. The theory that following abreaction one must act contrary to any feeling expressions that come from the past.

DEFENSE MECHANISMS. When a person fears that a personal defect will bring a painful loss of self-esteem and the ego unconsciously chooses some form of psychological defense.

DEFENSIVE DISCOUNTING. When a person defends against his own defects and inadequacies and seeks to relieve his anxiety by focusing on the inadequacies of others.

DENIAL. When the ego faces an external threat, stress or danger which it is unable to handle and simply denies the existence of the threat.

DEPRESSION. A state of despondency characterized by feelings of inadequacy, lowered activity and pessimism about the future.

DETERMINISM. The doctrine that human actions are the necessary results of antecedent causes.

DIRECTIVE COUNSELING. Counseling in which positive advice and interpretation are given.

DISCHARGE. The release of unconscious material, which is constantly trying to come to the surface.

DISPLACEMENT. The substitution of one response for another when the first is blocked, such as occurs in displaced aggression or hostility.

DISSOCIATION. When a whole complex pattern of psychological processes functions independently of the main stream of consciousness. The multiple personality illustrates this dissociation in its extreme form.

EGO. The self.

EGOISM. The striving for security by trying to organize the universe around oneself.

EMOTION. The psychosomatic form in which a person experiences his estimate of the beneficial or harmful relationships of some aspect of reality to himself.

EMOTIVE IMAGERY. A technique that accelerates the self-change process. It involves a person imagining himself in a situation in which he would ordinarily behave or emote in ways that he does not desire. He then pictures himself in that same situation behaving in the way he would like to behave.

ENDO-PSYCHIC WITHDRAWAL. The psychological withdrawing from an endeavor when one considers his goal to be unattainable.

FANTASY. The process of imagining objects or events in terms of imagery. It takes the form of both day and night dreaming.

FEELING EXPRESSIONS. The manifestations of one's feelings (sensations with meaning).

FLAGELLATION. The practice of submitting to whipping which is based upon the idea that suffering, in some magical way, atones for or nullifies evil.

HYSTERICAL DISORDER. A disorder that is characterized by emotional instability, repression, dissociation and suggestibility. Often mental conflicts are converted into physical symptoms such as paralyses, blindness, loss of voice and sleepwalking.

IDENTIFICATION. Seeking to acquire characteristics of a person one perceives to be adequate in order to find adequacy, power and status.

INCORPORATION. A form of seeking to identify oneself with someone he perceives as having adequacy, power and status. It is believed that another's whole psychic image can become part of his own individual personality.

INHIBITION. A mental blockage, a hesitancy to behave, particularly in a somewhat unconventional manner.

INSIGHT. The bringing to awareness of motives, relationships, feelings, impulses, etc., which previously had been poorly understood or of which the subject was totally unaware. It is making the unconscious to become conscious. It is a sudden glimpse of the obvious.

INSIGHT COUNSELING. The kind of counseling that deals with more than surface issues. It seeks to uncover psychological facts of which the counselee is unaware.

INTEGRATION. The process by which parts are unified into a whole. Each part of the personality works together in a smooth, coordinated manner.

INTELLECTUALIZATION. The overaccentuation and use of intellectual concepts and vocabulary to defend oneself against the anxiety associated with a particular experience or situation.

INTERNALIZATION. The incorporation of attitudes, standards of conduct, opinions, beliefs, etc., within the personality.

INTROJECTION. The symbolic assimilation of the loved or hated external object. Introjection has taken place when a child follows the standards and values of his parents not because he is told to do so but because he wants to, since he has become like his parents.

ISOLATION. Keeping apart that which belongs together.

LOGOTHERAPY. The kind of counseling that places an emphasis upon having meaning in one's life. It focuses upon the future rather than the past.

MORALISM. The view that man can live up to any ideal or law that is obligatory upon him. He fulfills what he ought to do by making the principles of reason and conscience triumph over the irrational and sensuous elements in his makeup.

MORAL RELATIVISM. The view that there are no moral absolutes, that principles of right and wrong are subject to change.

MORES. The traditional rules and customs of a group of people or a society. They are accepted as right and morally binding.

NARCISSISM. The excessive love or admiration of oneself.

NEOCORTEX. The thinking part of your brain.

NEUROSIS. An anxiety attack which may result from a multitude of causes. Modern psychiatric texts seem to be using the expression "anxiety attack" to replace the term "neurosis."

NEUROTIC. One who is expressing a chronic, nonspecific type of anxiety.

NOUTHETIC. The basis of this word is the Greek word *nouthesia* which has been translated "admonition" (KJV). It signifies putting people in mind of certain spiritual truths and realities.

OBSESSION-COMPULSION. An anxiety state characterized by persistent and often unwanted ideas (obsessions) and strong impulses to carry out irrational acts (compulsions).

OEDIPUS COMPLEX. According to Freud, a child's repressed desires for sexual intercourse with the parent of the opposite sex.

PARATAXIC DISTORTIONS. Any attitude toward another person based on fantasy or identification of that person with another figure.

PHENOMENOLOGY. The study of phenomena (things or events) as they actually occur immediately in experience without interpretation.

PHOBIC DISORDER. An intense fear of an object or situation intellectually recognized as not truly dangerous. It is the result of a displacement: one's unconscious fear of an original object or situation is attached symbolically to a new object—one that is within the individual's power to avoid.

PHYSIOLOGICAL. Having to do with natural physical functioning of an organism.

PLEASURE/PAIN SENSORY APPARATUS. The sensory apparatus of the human body that influences man to be governed by the search for pleasure and the avoidance of pain.

PROACTION. A belief that after one has relived the traumas of the past and has countered any feeling expressions that come from the past, he is to *proact* or express present feelings with present meanings.

PROJECTION. Attributing one's own traits or attitudes to others.

PSYCHE. The mind, including both conscious and unconscious processes.

PSYCHIATRY. The specialized branch of medicine that deals with the diagnosis, treatment and prevention of mental disorders.

PSYCHOANALYSIS. A form of psychotherapy that seeks the roots of human behavior in unconscious motivation and conflict. Freud placed much importance upon sex in a person's development. Many prominent psychoanalysts have greatly disagreed with the emphasis upon sex and have given much more importance to security and interpersonal relations. However, the technique of psychoanalysis has remained more or less unchanged. This technique involves free association and dream analysis over long periods of time in order to get at the sources of the unconscious impulses.

PSYCHODYNAMICS. The branch of psychology that is primarily concerned with investigating motivation and emotional processes.

PSYCHOLOGY. The study of the mind of man and the behavior of man and animals.

PSYCHOPATHOLOGY. The branch of psychology concerned with the investigation of mental disorders.

PSYCHOSIS. A severe mental disorder characterized by disorganization of the thought processes, disturbances in emotionality, disorientation as to time, space and person, and in some cases, hallucinations and delusions.

PSYCHOSOMATIC. The processes that are both somatic (bodily) and psychic (mental) in nature. It refers to the relation of mind and body.

PSYCHOTHERAPY. The application of specialized techniques to the treatment of emotional disorders.

RATIONAL BEHAVIOR THERAPY. A counseling technique that is based upon the fact that the ability to think logically enables people to better control their emotions and behavior.

RATIONAL EMOTIVE THERAPY. Another name for Rational Behavior Therapy. Albert Ellis called it Rational Emotive Therapy before it was renamed by Maxie Maultsby.

RATIONAL SELF-ANALYSIS. A self-help technique that enables a troubled person to logically analyze his thinking, feeling and behavior.

REACTION FORMATION. The development of a personality trait that is the opposite of the original, unconscious or repressed trait. For example, a mother who unconsciously rejects her child may become overprotective of the child.

REFERRAL. The act of sending a patient or client to an agency or individual for further treatment or consultation.

REGRESSION. Returning to an earlier level of development so that primitive levels of behavior are seen in older individuals.

REPRESSION. The forceful ejection from consciousness of impulses, memories or experiences that are painful or shameful and generate a high level of anxiety.

SCHIZOPHRENIA. A general name for a group of psychotic reactions. It involves the mind splitting from reality. Schizophrenics may see things others do not see or hear things others do not hear. It is usually accompanied by negativistic behavior.

SELF-ACTUALIZATION. The tendency to develop one's personality, talents and capacities.

SELF-ESTEEM. The individual's evaluation of himself.

SHOCK THERAPY. The treatment of mental disorders by passing an electric current through the brain or by the administration of drugs that induce convulsions.

SITUATION ETHICS. A belief that the rightness or wrongness of an action can be influenced by the situation or circumstances.

SOLIPSIST. One who believes that only his own experience can be known to him.

SOMATIC. That which pertains to the body.

SUBLIMATION. Any redirection of socially unacceptable impulses into acceptable channels.

SUBSTITUTION. The replacing of one goal with another when the route to the first goal has been blocked.

SYMBOLIZATION. The mechanism by which one idea or object is used to represent another. It defends against anxiety because we can tolerate the symbol chosen without experiencing significant degrees of anxiety. This mechanism is utilized in phobias.

TEMPERAMENT. A person's nature or disposition.

THERAPEUTIC. That which is curative in function.

TRANSFERANCE. In general, any displacement of feeling from one object to another. Sometimes feelings toward another become directed toward the counselor.

UNCONSCIOUS. The unconscious mind. A storehouse of repressed feelings, fears and desires that the conscious mind usually cannot call up at will.

UNCOVERING TECHNIQUES. Techniques used for the purpose of bringing the unconscious to the surface where it can be faced realistically and, in the Christian sense, Scripturally.

UNDOING. A defense mechanism whereby the individual engages in a ritual or symbolic act which is intended to abolish the effect of an act previously completed.

VALUES. The established ideals of life.

VERBALIZING. A statement or expression in the form of words.

Bibliography

Books

Adams, Jay E. *Competent to Counsel.* Grand Rapids: Baker Book House, 1970.

Backus, William, and Marie Chapian. *Telling Yourself the Truth.* Minneapolis: Bethany House, 1980.

Branden, Nathaniel. *The Psychology of Self-Esteem.* Los Angeles: Nash Publishing Corporation, 1969.

——————— *The Disowned Self.* Los Angeles: Nash Publishing Corporation, 1971.

Burns, David D. *Feeling Good.* New York: William Morrow and Co., 1980.

Calabrese, Alphonse, and William Proctor. *RX: The Christian Love-Treatment.* Garden City, NY: Doubleday & Co., 1976.

Chaplin, J. P. *Dictionary of Psychology.* New York: Dell Publishing Co., 1968.

Clinebell, Howard J., Jr. *Basic Types of Pastoral Counseling.* Nashville: Abingdon Press, 1966.

Collins, Gary. *How to be a People Helper.* Santa Ana, CA: Vision House, 1976.

Collins, Vincent P. *Me, Myself and You.* St. Meinrad, IN: Abbey Press, 1973.

Cramer, Raymond L. *The Psychology of Jesus & Mental Health.* Grand Rapids: Zondervan Publishing House, 1959.

Dobson, James. *Hide or Seek.* Old Tappan, NJ: Fleming H. Revell Co., 1974.

Drakeford, John W. *Integrity Therapy.* Nashville: Broadman Press, 1961.

Ellis, Albert, and Robert A. Harper. *A New Guide to Rational Living.* Englewood Cliffs, NJ: Prentice-Hall, 1975.

Fenichel, Otto. *The Psychoanalytic Theory of Neurosis.* New York: W. W. Norton & Co., 1945.

Fitts, William H. *The Experience of Psychotherapy*. Princeton, NJ: D. Van Nostrand Co., 1965.

Fletcher, Joseph. *Situation Ethics*. Philadelphia: The Westminster Press, MEMLXVI.

Frankl, Viktor E. *Man's Search for Meaning*. Washington Square Press editions. New York: Washington Square Press, 1963.

Friedman, Meyer, and Ray H. Rosenman. *Type A Behavior And Your Heart*. New York: Alfred A. Knopf, 1974.

Glasser, William. *Reality Therapy, A New Approach to Psychiatry*. New York: Harper & Row, 1975.

Goodman, David S., and Maxie C. Maultsby, Jr. *Emotional Well-Being Through Rational Behavior Training*. Springfield, IL: Charles C. Thomas, 1974.

Greenwald, Harold. *Decision Therapy*. New York: Peter Wyden, Inc. 1973. Greenwald encourages counselees to look back on their lives to discover which life choices or decisions are behind their present problems. He helps them to explore the alternatives and to choose one that they think is most likely to relieve their distress.

Gross, Martin L. *The Psychological Society*. New York: Random House, 1978.

Haas, Harold J. *Pastoral Counseling*. St. Louis: Concordia Publishing House, 1970.

Harper, Robert A. *Psychoanalysis and Psychotherapy, 36 Systems*. Englewood Cliffs, NJ: Prentice-Hall, 1959.

Hauck, Paul A. *Overcoming Frustration and Anger*. Philadelphia: The Westminster Press, 1974. The RBT approach is used to deal with the particular problems of frustration and anger.

__________. *Reason in Pastoral Counseling*. Philadelphia: The Westminster Press, 1982.

Hyde, Margaret O., and Edward S. Marks. *Psychology in Action*. 2d ed. New York: McGraw-Hill Book Co., 1976.

Hyder, O. Quentin. *The Christian's Handbook of Psychiatry*. Old Tappan, NJ: Fleming H. Revell Co., 1971.

Jeeves, Malcolm A. *Psychology & Christianity: The View Both Ways*. Downers Grove, IL: InterVarsity Press, 1977.

Jourard, Sidney M. *The Transparent Self*. New York: Van Nostrand Reinhold Co., 1971.

Kovel, Joel. *A Complete Guide to Therapy from Psychoanalysis to Behavior Modification*. New York: Pantheon Books, 1976.

Lair, Jess. *I Ain't Much, Baby—But I'm All I've Got*. Garden City, NY: Doubleday & Co., 1969.

Layden, Milton. *Escaping the Hostility Trap*. Englewood Cliffs, NJ: Prentice-Hall, 1977.

Liebman, Monte H. *Introduction to Psychotherapy*. Brookfield, WI: Med-Psyche Publications, 1977.

Lloyd-Jones, D. Martyn. *Spiritual Depression: Its Cause and Cure*. Grand Rapids: Wm. B. Eerdmans Pub. Co., 1965.

Mallory, James D. *The Kink & I*. Wheaton, IL: Victor Books, 1973. The insights of psychiatry are used in applying the resources of God's Word to emotional problems.

Matson, Katinka. *The Psychology Today Omnibook of Personal Development*. New York: William Morrow and Co., 1977.

Maultsby, Maxie C., Jr. *Handbook of Rational Self-Counseling*. Lexington: The Rational Behavior Training Section, University of Kentucky Medical Center, 1971.

——————— . *Help Yourself to Happiness*. New York: Institute for Rational Living, Inc., 1975.

Maultsby, Maxie C., Jr., and Allie Hendricks. *You and Your Emotions*. Lexington: University of Kentucky Medical Center, 1974.

May, Rollo. *The Courage to Create*. New York: W.W. Norton & Co., 1975.

McCall, Raymond J. *The Varieties of Abnormality*. Springfield, IL: Charles C. Thomas, 1975.

Morris, Paul D. *Love Therapy*. Wheaton, IL: Tyndale House Publishers, 1974.

Oakes, Wayne E. *The Psychology of Religion*. Waco, TX: Word Books, 1973.

Osborn, Cecil. *The Art of Understanding Yourself*. Grand Rapids: Zondervan Books, 1967. A rare combination of religious insight and psychological truth. It deals specifically with the themes of alienation from self and determinism.

Outler, Albert C. *Psychotherapy and the Christian Message*. New York: Harper & Row, 1954.

Roberts, David E. *Psychotherapy and a Christian View of Man*. New York: Charles Scribner's Sons, 1950.

Rubin, Theodore J. *The Angry Book*. New York: Mcmillan Co., 1969. Rubin describes the many self-deceiving ways in which people handle anger.

Schomp, Gerald. *Overcoming Anxiety*. Cincinnati: St. Anthony Messenger Press, 1976.

Sire, James. *The Universe Next Door: A Basic World View Catalog*. Downers Grove, IL: InterVarsity Press, 1976.

Solomon, Charles R. *Counseling With the Mind of Christ. The Dynamics of Spirituotherapy*. Old Tappan, NJ: Fleming H. Revell, 1977.

Tournier, Paul. *The Best of Paul Tournier*. New York: Iverson–Norman Associates, 1977.

White, Robert W. *The Abnormal Personality*. New York: The Ronald Press, 1956.

Wilson, Colin. *New Pathways in Psychology: Maslow & the Post-Freudian Revolution*. London: Victor Gollancz, 1972.

Wright, H. Norman. *The Christian Use of Emotional Power*. Old Tappan, NJ: Fleming H. Revell Co., 1974. Wright shows how through reading the Scriptures and letting the Holy Spirit work in our lives, we can abandon all old thought patterns which are at the root of negative emotions.

Periodicals

Jackson, Basil. "Psychology, Psychiatry and the Pastor." *Bibliotheca Sacra* 1 & 2 (1975).

Mitchell, Norman L. *Ministry* (May 1982).

Radcliff, J.D. "I Am Joe's Brain." *Reader's Digest* (April 1974).

Roszak, Theodore. "Getting Your Head Together." *Newsweek* (September 6, 1976).

Stone, Marvin. "Our Solipsist Society." *U.S. News and World Report* (September 5, 1978).

Miscellaneous Sources

Cole, Edward. Statement in class. California Graduate School of Theology, Milwaukee extension, October 1978.

Duvall, Nancy. Business and professional seminar. Rosemead, CA, 1976.

Ellison, Craig W., ed. *Self-Esteem*. First in a series of monographs to be published entitled "Christian Perspectives on Counseling and the Behavioral Sciences." Oklahoma City: Southwestern Press for Christian Association for Psychological Studies, 1976.

Hart, Joseph. "Feeling Therapy." An abstract published by the Center for Feeling, 1017 South LaBrea Ave., Los Angeles, 1978.

Jackson, Basil. Lecture at California Graduate School of Theology, Milwaukee extension, November 8, 1978.

__________ . "Repression." Class hand-out paper. California Graduate School of Theology, Milwaukee extension, 1978.

__________ . "Categories of Mental Symptoms." Class hand-out paper. California Graduate School of Theology, Milwaukee extension, 1978.

__________ . Personal interview. Milwaukee, 1978.

Maultsby, Maxie C., Jr. REI Script Format. Lexington: University of Kentucky College of Medicine, 1976.

Mowrer, O. Hobart. Address at the Convocation of Religion-in-Life Week at Iowa State University, January 20, 1960.

Index